LEVITICUS BIBLE STUDY

A COMPANION TO

Leviticus: An Introduction and Commentary

SCOTT BEHM

AND JAY SKLAR

ISBN: 978-1-7323057-0-0

ACKNOWLEDGEMENTS

Scott worked as a lawyer on the West Coast for more than 20 years before he and his family decided to move across the country to St. Louis so he could attend Covenant Theological Seminary. There he met Jay, who taught at the seminary and who—for reasons most people don't understand—had a deep love for Leviticus. After Scott graduated, they worked together on this study for more than a year, with Scott doing the lion's share of the work, writing first drafts of each lesson that were so good, Jay barely had to edit them. (Scott asked that the preceding line be omitted, but Jay insisted otherwise, and since Jay is the professor, he won.)

Jay would like to thank Scott for his fantastic work on this and thank Cheryl Eaton, also a Covenant graduate, for her fine copy editing at the very end of the process. He is forever indebted to his wife, Ski, who (once again) listened patiently and joyfully to lots of talk about Leviticus while this Bible study was being prepared.

Scott, in turn, would like to thank Jay for the opportunity to help express the truths of Leviticus in this Bible study, using learning methods he studied at Covenant. Jay's optimism about the giftedness of others—even if sometimes misplaced—is a huge encouragement to them to persevere! Scott also wants to thank Wendy, his perpetually faithful wife, who encouraged him each week that this study will bless the Church and who also focus-tested several lessons with her young women's Bible study.

TABLE OF CONTENTS

INTRODUCTION

This guide is a companion to Jay Sklar, *Leviticus: An Introduction and Commentary*, Tyndale Old Testament Commentary Series, Vol. 3 (Downers Grove, IL: InterVarsity Press, 2014). You will need a copy of the commentary to use this study. The commentary is available at Amazon.com and other publishers. (Note: Jay has also written a longer commentary on Leviticus that will be published by Zondervan; this study assumes you have the InterVarsity Press commentary.)

As you begin this study, it is important to consider the following question: Are you willing to give Leviticus a chance?

This may seem to be an unusual question to ask at the start of a Bible study, but for most people, Leviticus is a very unusual book. For some, the litany of laws and details are either overwhelming or utterly boring. For others, the topics it discusses—from sacrifice to skin diseases to bodily discharges—are off-putting. When we add the passages that describe the Lord's judgment, bizarre cultural realities that make no sense to us (such as ritual impurity), and a sexual ethic often at odds with Western cultural assumptions, Leviticus is not just unusual, it is problematic. There seems to be little hope of attracting modern readers to it.

But what if Leviticus actually answers some of the deepest questions we have as human beings, such as "What is our purpose? What is life all about? Where can I find hope?" What if Leviticus is a central part of a grand narrative that describes where we can find meaning? What if it sets out a vision for human flourishing that meets our heart's deepest longings?

I believe we will find that Leviticus does all these things—if we are willing to give it the chance.

Why we struggle with Leviticus

While we struggle with Leviticus for many specific reasons, I believe they can be grouped into three categories.

First, we usually do not see Leviticus as part of an amazing story that casts an incredible vision. And yet it is. In creation, the Lord, as heavenly King:

- placed humans in a lush garden,
- walked in fellowship with them,
- gave them a Sabbath rest, and

- made them in his image so that they might reflect his character into all the world, making it a place shining with his goodness, justice, mercy, and love.

In Leviticus, this same heavenly King comes to:
- lead the Israelites to a lush land flowing with milk and honey,
- "walk" in their midst in his holy Tent (Lev 26:11-12),
- give them Sabbath rest, and
- call them to embody his goodness, justice, mercy, and love so that the world may again shine with these things.

The parallels are clear. "Simply put, the Israelites are not only to be a signpost back to Eden; they are to become a manifestation of it and a people who extend Eden's borders to every corner of the earth" (p. 29; see further pp. 27-30 [§1], 54-55 [§4.h]).

This vision should resonate deeply with those who follow Jesus, not only because he calls us to reflect God's character into all the world and spread his kingdom to every corner of the earth, but also because his word assures us he will bring about this vision fully and finally. "In the book of Revelation, the Bible concludes by telling us that a day is coming when King Jesus will fill this entire world fully and completely with his kingdom. It is a day in which heaven comes to earth, when we can eat freely of the fruit of the tree of life, when there will be no more death or mourning or crying or pain, when the curse of Eden will be fully and finally destroyed, and the blessing of Eden will be experienced by all those who follow Jesus as King (Rev. 21:1–5; 22:1–5). This is the day the people of King Jesus work for, long for and pray for (1 Cor. 1:7; Phil. 3:20; 2 Pet. 3:12). It is a day of such glory and grace that they cannot help but cry, 'Amen. Come, Lord Jesus' (Rev. 22:20)" (pp. 75-76; see further pp. 74-76 [§6c]).

The second overarching reason we struggle with Leviticus is that many of its values clash with our own. More on that below.

Third, Leviticus is a struggle because we do not understand many of the cultural realities and issues it addresses. This should not surprise us: Leviticus was written more than three thousand years ago to a nomadic people wandering in the wilderness near Israel. Their world was radically different than ours. For them, animal sacrifice was common (Lev 1-7). Their worship center was a portable tent around which they camped and where priests ministered in ornate uniforms (Lev 8). Issues of ritual purity and impurity were cultural realities (Lev 11-15). Many people today, however, have never seen an animal sacrifice. Our worship centers (if we have them) are buildings often outside our neighborhoods, where many pastors dress informally, never mind in clerical robes, and issues of ritual purity and impurity are completely unknown. While this makes reading a book such as Leviticus challenging, it does not make it impossible, especially if we keep a few tips in mind.

Five tips for reading Leviticus well

First, the Lord is addressing Israelites in the book of Leviticus, and he speaks to them in a way that *they* can understand. Because they lived at a different time and place than we do, some of the ways he speaks to them and some of the things he speaks to them about will seem strange to us. We must resist the temptation to sit in judgment on these things or simply dismiss them; instead, we must seek to understand, "What would this have meant to an ancient Israelite?" *I find this one of the most important tips to keep in mind when reading this book.* For example, we read about ritual purity and impurity in many places in Leviticus and can be tempted to think, "That's just strange; why in the world include such bizarre laws?" But ritual purity and impurity were common cultural realities in Israel's day, and the Lord weaves this reality into the laws of Leviticus to teach the Israelites important lessons concerning his holiness, his desire for them to reflect his holy character, and the importance of doing so in all of life (see pp. 44-49 [§4.f], esp. pp. 48-49 [§4.f.iv]). These lessons would have made good sense to the Israelites, whether or not they are immediately apparent to us. This should remind us when we come across something in Leviticus that strikes us as strange, our first response should be to stop and ask, "How would an Israelite have understood this?" (For more on this see pp. 55-57 [§5a] of the Introduction.)

Second, as you read, remember Leviticus is part of a larger story in which the heavenly King (the Lord) has come down to dwell in his royal palace (the Tent of Meeting) in the midst of the people (the Israelites) he has rescued in his love that they might have fellowship with him. Keeping that picture in mind will give you the right framework for understanding what you are reading. What are the sacrifices? Opportunities for the Israelites to come to the palace of their heavenly King, either to reconcile with him for breaking his laws or to give him honor for his greatness and loving grace (Leviticus 1-7). Who are the priests? Servants of this King, working in his palace-tent, teaching the King's people his laws, guiding them into his presence for worship, and seeking the King's favor and blessing on the people's behalf (Leviticus 8-10). We could go on, but the point is clear: Leviticus is the story of the heavenly King in the midst of the people he has redeemed in love that they might have fellowship with him. (For more on this see pp. 27-29 [§1].)

Third, this King is not simply dwelling among his people, he is also forming them into a kingdom in which his character—his justice, mercy, goodness, and love—are to be on full display. The laws play a crucial role here since laws reflect the values of the lawgiver. We understand this intuitively: Our society has laws against murder because we value life. Similarly, the "laws" that good parents give their children are based on certain values they want their children to learn: the importance of speaking the truth, of respecting others, of not causing people harm. In the same way, the laws of Leviticus are an expression of the Lord's values, and he gives them to the Israelites to shape them into a people who reflect those values into the world. Why command his people that instead of holding a grudge, they are to forgive and love their neighbors as themselves (Lev 19:18)? To teach them the importance of showing to others the same mercy and love they have received from him. Why forbid partiality in the courts (Lev 19:15)? To teach that all people bear his image equally and are worthy of equal justice. Why have a year of Jubilee, with its economic reset that delivers people from crushing debt (Lev 25:8-10)? To teach the importance of care for the less fortunate (and that material gain is not all there is in life). These laws are meant to shape the Lord's people into those who embody his character in the world. (For more on this see pp. 41-42 [§4.d].)

This leads naturally to the fourth point: While not every law in Leviticus applies today, the laws still have something to teach us because they are based on the Lord's values. For example, laws about atoning sacrifices no longer apply because Jesus is the final and ultimate atoning sacrifice. No more are needed (Heb 10:12). But studying laws about atoning sacrifices still has much to teach us, such as: Our sin separates us from a holy God and must be made right; God in his love and grace provides us with a way to deal with our wrong so that we might be made right with him; sacrifices must be pure and blameless if they are to atone for sin. Indeed, understanding these lessons in Leviticus actually helps us to understand Jesus' sacrificial work with greater clarity—and far deeper appreciation. (The more I have studied sacrifice in Leviticus, the more meaningful and beautiful the Lord's Supper has become to me.) In short, instead of skipping over these laws because they belong to the Old Testament or have been fulfilled in Jesus, we should approach them expectantly and with a desire to understand the deeper values on which they are based because these are the Lord's values. To put it more strongly: These laws serve as a window into God's heart and therefore deserve our earnest study and reflection. (For more on this and on distinguishing between those laws that apply today and those that do not, see pp. 57-62 [§5.b].)

Finally, because these laws reflect the Lord's character, they will often challenge the cultural assumptions you and I bring to the text. His character is the standard when it comes to that which is good and just. This is what makes him "holy," which is the biblical way of describing how utterly unique and distinct he is when it comes to goodness and uprightness and justice and love. No cultural system overlaps with his holy values perfectly. Every culture has some assumptions that align with the Lord's holy values and those that do not. Some cultures place a high priority on forgiveness over vengeance, in which case it will make good sense reading the Lord's commands, "Do not seek revenge or bear a grudge against anyone among your people, but love your neighbor as yourself" (Lev 19:18). In other cultures, where vengeance takes priority, this command will seem bizarre and make no intuitive sense. At such points, we must seriously ask ourselves, "Am I willing to let my conscience and intuitions be more influenced by God's Word than by my surrounding culture?"

In many Western contexts, the example I just gave is perhaps not too difficult, since Western cultures often highly value love and forgiveness, making it easier to agree that God's word should shape our conscience and intuition in such matters. More challenging, perhaps, are examples involving sexual ethics. In some cultures, every aspect of the sexual ethic laid out in Leviticus 18 will make sense, whereas in others (such as most modern Western cultures), parts of the sexual ethic will make sense (such as the prohibition against incest), but other parts will not (such as the prohibition against homosexual activity). Once again, the question remains: "Am I willing to let my conscience and intuitions be more influenced by God's word than by my surrounding culture?" I encourage you as you work through this book, or any book of the Bible, to make it your prayer, "O Lord, please protect me from trying to form you into my image so that I end up worshipping myself. Instead, use your Word to form me into your image so that I end up worshipping you as you truly are!"

How to Use This Study

As noted above (Introduction), this guide is a companion to Jay Sklar, *Leviticus: An Introduction and Commentary*, Tyndale Old Testament Commentary Series, Vol. 3 (Downers Grove, IL: InterVarsity Press, 2014). You will need a copy of the commentary to use this study. In terms of the study itself, the following observations will help you to use it most effectively.

Individual and Group Study

The study guide is designed to facilitate a weekly individual and group study. Although you can work through this study of Leviticus on your own, we strongly recommend that you participate with a small group of friends in your church community. If you're not a Christian, or if you don't have a church family, we recommend that you complete the study with a few Christian friends. God has revealed his word to us as a people, not as individuals, so he desires that we come to know him better and grow deeper in relationship with him as part of a community. From a practical perspective, working through this study and growing deeper in your understanding of a difficult book such as Leviticus will be much easier and more rewarding if you pursue it with others. However, if you choose to do the study on your own, the questions in the Group Study will certainly enrich your time by adding to or reinforcing the applications in the Individual Study.

Course of Study

This guide is designed generally to facilitate a 29-week study period, working through the commentary Introduction and each chapter or section of Leviticus, roughly one chapter/section per week. The 29-week study will take most groups a year to complete, from September through May. For groups not able to accommodate a full 29-week study, we've designed a number of shorter topical studies of 12 weeks. Consult "Options for Study Series" below if your group is interested in pursuing one of these shorter studies.

Weekly Readings

Each week, the guide will direct you to read a passage of Leviticus for that lesson. We recommend that you read the passage at least twice and take notes on any questions you may have. Because the historical, cultural, and literary context of a Scripture passage (or any text) is so important to understanding its meaning, the study guide will also direct you to read a "Context" section in the commentary relating to the passage and sometimes background readings in the commentary's Introduction. Then, as you begin working through questions in the study guide, you will be directed to read "Comment" sections in the commentary relating to specific verses in the passage. Some students may benefit from reading the entire commentary section corresponding to the Leviticus passage for that lesson and then re-reading specific "Context," "Comment," and Introduction sections as directed by each part of the lesson.

Individual Study

The first part of each lesson is the Individual Study, divided into three sections.

- The "Engage" section connects the lesson's key theme with your life through an initial reflection question. It then directs you to the Scripture, "Context," and Introduction readings.
- The "Understand" section leads you through a series of questions to reinforce information you have learned from the Scripture and commentary "Comment" readings.
- The "Apply/Respond" section helps you apply what you have learned in Leviticus to the New Testament and to life in general. In particular, the prompts to "Meditate" and "Take Action" help move your new learning from your head to your heart and hands.

The Individual Study will take an hour or so of your time each week. Some students may benefit most from a single study session. Others may choose to break the Individual Study into two or more sessions. You can also divide it into three sessions, for example, with the "Engage" section as session one, "Understand" as session two, and "Apply/Respond" as session three.

Group Study

The second part of each lesson is the Group Study. Each lesson is meant to facilitate a group meeting time of about 50 minutes. The lessons provide suggested time allocations for each part of the Group Study. You can adjust these times, of course, for your particular needs, such as fellowship, prayer, or worship. You'll notice the directions on the first page of each Group Study are the same for each lesson. This is meant to provide a consistent rhythm across the lessons. But you should feel free to modify any of these elements to meet specific desires for your group. Some groups, for example, may prefer to have spontaneous opening prayer, rather than using the prayer suggested in the lesson. Some groups may prefer to not break into pairs to share reflections from the Individual Study; others may decide not to share reflections at all.

The application questions in the Group Study typically differ from those in the Individual Study. In some cases, however, they are meant to enhance and reinforce certain application questions from the Individual Study.

The Group Study ends with a prompt called "Evaluate" or "Create." These are meant to give your group "action items" for application beyond your gathering times. These are merely suggestions related to each particular lesson; your group should feel free to modify them in ways that may be more pertinent to your group, community or church.

May the Lord richly bless your study of Leviticus!

OPTIONS FOR STUDY SERIES

The table below describes seven 12-week study series for churches or small groups that are not able to complete the full 29-lesson series in this Study Guide. **For those wanting a 10-week study, skip the lessons marked with an asterisk.**

1. Understanding Leviticus
2. The Gospel in Leviticus
3. Jesus in Leviticus
4. Sacrifice and Worship in Leviticus
5. Holiness in Leviticus
6. Community and Ministry in Leviticus
7. Ethics and Mission in Leviticus

UNDERSTANDING LEVITICUS

WEEK	TOPIC	TITLE OF LESSON	PAGE
1	Introductory matters	Context, Theology, Special Issues, and Jesus' Fulfillment of Leviticus	p. 13
2	Sacrifice	The Burnt Offering – Lev. 1	p. 21
3	Sacrifice	The Fellowship Offering – Lev. 3	p. 35
4	Sacrifice	The Purification Offering – Lev. 4	p. 44
5	Sacrifice	The Reparation Offering – Lev. 5:14–6:7	p. 58
6	Priests	Ordination of the Priests for Public Worship – Lev. 8	p. 87
7*	Purity	Further Laws on Ritually Defiling Body Fluids – Lev. 15	p. 130
8	Day of Atonement	The Day of Atonement – Lev. 16	p. 137
9	Living as a kingdom of priests: worship and sexuality	Laws Against Certain Sex and Worship Practices – Lev. 18	p. 153
10*	Living as a kingdom of priests: worship and sexuality	Consequences for Illicit Sexual and Spiritual Practices – Lev. 20	p. 170
11	Living as a kingdom of priests: ethics and God's mission	The Lord's Holy Practices for His Holy People – Lev. 19	p. 162
12	Living as a kingdom of priests: ethics and God's mission	Covenant Blessings and Curses – Lev. 26	p. 216

THE GOSPEL IN LEVITICUS

JESUS IN LEVITICUS

SACRIFICE AND WORSHIP IN LEVITICUS

HOLINESS IN LEVITICUS

COMMUNITY AND MINISTRY IN LEVITICUS

ETHICS AND MISSION IN LEVITICUS

| INTRODUCTION |

CONTEXT, THEOLOGY, SPECIAL ISSUES, AND JESUS' FULFILLMENT OF LEVITICUS

ENGAGE

Reflect

As you prepare to study Leviticus, it's helpful to be aware of any **preconceptions** or **questions** about the book that you may bring. So before you begin, spend a few minutes reflecting on your current understanding of Leviticus and jot down a few notes:

When I think about the book of Leviticus, I think:

Questions I have that I hope this study answers:

Pray

Heavenly Father, as I study Leviticus, I pray that you would give me an accurate understanding of your word, especially what it means for my fellowship with you, the mission of your church on earth, and your grace and mercy to those who believe and are saved through the sacrifice of our great high priest, your Son Jesus, in whose name I pray. Amen.

Read

- In the "Introduction" to the Commentary, read Sections 1 (27-30), and 4-6 (37-76). Note: this first lesson involves more reading than the others. If your time is short, skip any questions with a *.
- As you read these introductory sections, write down any questions that occur to you in the margins or on a separate sheet of paper. If you are studying with a group, you can raise these questions for consideration when you meet to discuss this lesson.

A. Context (27-30)

1. Many people today, including Christians, may view the laws of Leviticus as burdensome. But the ancient Israelites were to look on them as a blessing, as life-giving instructions that answered life's most important question. What is that question (28)?

2. In Leviticus, the Lord *separated* his people from other peoples of the earth to reflect his image and *blessed* them in many ways, most importantly by dwelling among them as their God. He then *called* them to reflect his image in the world, thus representing him on earth and fulfilling his purpose for humanity. What were the Israelites called to show the rest of the world (29)?

B. The Theology of Leviticus (37-55)

1. Briefly identify at least three factors in Leviticus that indicate the tabernacle was not simply a tent, but the palace-tent of the heavenly King dwelling in the people's midst (37):

2. The covenant between the Lord and Israel has implications for ancient Israel and for modern readers. In your own words, briefly describe these two implications (38):

    • For ancient Israel:

    • For modern readers:

*   3. To be holy is to be *set apart* as distinct in some way. Briefly describe two ways by which the Lord set apart his people in Leviticus (39). (Remember: if time is short, skip any questions with a *.)

*   4. The Pentateuch (the Bible's first five books) focuses on two important aspects of God's *independent* holiness—that is, his holiness *by nature*. What are these two aspects in which the Lord is completely distinct from every other being in the universe (39-40)?

*   5. To be redeemed by the Lord, the King of the universe, always implies relationship and relationship with him always implies mission. Briefly describe the nature of Israel's mission and how the Israelites were to accomplish it (41):

    6. The laws of Leviticus were stipulations of the covenant between the Lord and Israel. While modern people often view biblical law negatively, such was <u>not</u> the case for the faithful in ancient Israel. Briefly describe in your own words two important reasons for Israel's positive view of the law (41-42):

*   7. The essence of sin is to break the Lord's laws instead of keeping them. The results are always catastrophic. What are the results of sin, both for sinners and for the world (42)?

    8. Leviticus deals with both sin and ritual impurity. Sin is rooted in *moral wrong-doing*; impurity is not. Sin is an *action*; impurity is a *state of being*. In ancient Israel, there were three ritual states: holy, pure, and

impure (or holy, clean, and unclean) (44-45). What two things did the ritual states guide the community in understanding?

9. Although the *rationale* behind Israel's ritual states is difficult to know, we can be certain of at least three *purposes*. Briefly describe in your own words those three purposes (48-49):

*   10. The Lord graciously provided the Israelites with a means for forgiveness of their sins and cleansing from ritual impurity—*atonement*. While atonement served to purify or cleanse ritual impurity (51), it also served as a *ransom* for sin. Summarize in one or two sentences the biblical characteristics of ransom (50):

*   11. For reasons the text does not explain, the blood of a sacrificial animal was considered to be the most powerful purifying agent for ritual impurity in ancient Israel. The blood also served as a ransom payment for the guilt of sin (53). Yet atonement as a means of ransom and forgiveness was a gift from the Lord himself. How does this "turn the idea of sacrifice on its head" as the opposite of our common impulse concerning salvation (54)?

C. Special Issues in Leviticus (55-72)

1. The concept of *accommodation* helps modern readers to understand some of the laws in Leviticus that initially may strike us as strange. Accommodation refers to the fact that the Lord communicates his values using the cultural realities, practices, and customs of those to whom he is communicating (55-56). The notion of ritual states in ancient Near Eastern cultures is one example (56). But what does accommodation <u>not</u> mean (57)?

2. While many of the laws in Leviticus are no longer in effect, they all express the values of the law-giver: the Lord. Those values remain valid and are to be lived out by God's people today. The laws themselves can be grouped into four categories (chart, 58). The first are laws still in effect today because they are repeated in the New Testament (59). Briefly state why laws in the other three categories are no longer in effect (59-61):

* 3. Leviticus often does not explain the *meaning* of various ritual actions, probably because the Israelites already knew them. But the text is usually clear about the overall *purpose* of a given ritual. Knowing a ritual's purpose helps us to understand the meaning of actions within it. The Commentary gives the example of a wedding ceremony (70). Briefly explain how knowing that ceremony's purpose makes sense of its details:

* 4. Leviticus is clear that sacrificial atonement resulted in the Israelites' sins being forgiven. Yet the book of Hebrews is also clear that it is impossible for the blood of sacrificial animals to take away sins (Heb 10:4) The Commentary offers an analogy to help explain this apparent contradiction (72). Briefly explain the analogy in your own words:

D. Leviticus and the NT: the "How much more" of Jesus (72-76)

1. Leviticus teaches four points concerning atonement: (a) it was made by priests who presented sacrifices on the people's behalf; (b) the sacrifices both ransomed and cleansed sinners; (c) because individuals repeatedly sinned, the sacrifices for sin had to be continually repeated, as did the Day of Atonement once each year for the community's sins; and (d) atonement was not earned by the Israelites but granted by the Lord as a gracious gift (73). Briefly describe in your own words how Jesus fulfills each point in an ultimate and final way (73-74):

2. A key theme in Leviticus is the Lord *dwelling among his people* in the tabernacle. Briefly describe two ways the New Testament depicts Jesus as God dwelling among his people (74):

3. As we've seen, Leviticus casts a vision for God's people to return to his purposes for humanity in creation: to be a holy people reflecting God's character and, in this way, spreading his kingdom of goodness, justice, mercy, and love throughout the world (74). In what two ways does Jesus cast this same vision in the New Testament for his followers (75)?

4. The New Testament depicts Jesus as the King appointed over God's kingdom, demonstrating his distinct power and moral purity in remarkable ways. What do these demonstrations imply with regard to "the return to Eden" (75)?

5. In light of Jesus' fulfillment of God's purposes for his people as revealed in Leviticus, what is the call of the New Testament (75)?

CONTEXT, THEOLOGY, SPECIAL ISSUES, AND JESUS' FULFILLMENT OF LEVITICUS

——— ANALYZE ———

Opening Prayer

Heavenly Father, as we study Leviticus, we pray that you would give us an accurate understanding of your word, especially what it means for our fellowship with you, the mission of your church on earth, and your grace and mercy to those who believe and are saved through the sacrifice of our great high priest, your Son Jesus, in whose name we pray. Amen.

Share Reflections | 10 min.

Either in pairs or the large group, have participants share one or two reflections from the first page of the Individual Study. This is not a time to critique or ask a lot of questions of each other, but to share what God has put on your hearts concerning this lesson.

Clarify Issues from the Lesson | 20 min.

Spend time in the large group helping to clarify any uncertainties concerning the readings from the "Introduction" to the Commentary or the questions in the Individual Study. Use the space below and on the next page for notes:

——— EVALUATE ———

Jesus and the Return to Eden | 20 min.

We have seen that Leviticus casts a vision for the people of God to return to his purposes for humanity in creation: to be holy people reflecting his character and, in this way, spreading his kingdom of goodness, justice, mercy, and love throughout the world. Jesus casts this same vision in the New Testament, commanding his followers to pray for his kingdom to come and for God's will to "be done on earth as it is in heaven" (Mt. 6:10) (74-75). **Discuss some concrete ways in which your church or study group might reflect more deeply the character of Jesus and thereby participate even more fully in God's mission of bringing goodness, justice, mercy, and love into the world.**

THE BURNT OFFERING

ENGAGE

Reflect

Look at your calendar for the coming week. How many appointments are you anticipating because they offer opportunities for learning and growth? What about the others? Which of the people you are scheduled to meet are wise and following hard after Jesus? Which are not? Does your calendar include a regular meeting with the Lord—a private time and space where you can intimately experience his presence? Why or why not? Are you aware that right now, during this study, you are meeting with the Lord? Are you aware of his presence now and at other times during your day?

Pray

Heavenly Father, as I study your word in Leviticus, which you gave through your servant Moses with whom you met face-to-face as a friend, teach me through the Holy Spirit about right worship and what your instructions to ancient Israel mean for me and the community with whom I worship. In Jesus' name I pray and give you thanks. Amen.

Read

- Read Leviticus 1, which concerns the burnt offering. Keep in mind its purpose was to provide atonement—that is, forgiveness—for the worshippers and to underscore their prayers and praises. See "Context" chart (88).
- In the commentary, read "Introduction" sections 4.g.i (50), 4.g.v-4.h (54), 5.e (71-72), and "Context" (85, 87-89).
- Read Leviticus 1 again.

A. Tent of Meeting—Read "Comment" on Lev. 1:1 (86-87).

1. What was the significance of the "tent of meeting" in terms of the presence and revelation of the Lord?

2. In what way did the tent of meeting represent a royal palace in terms of the Lord's relationship with Israel?

3. What two things does Lev. 1:1-3 say happened at the tent of meeting?

B. Significance of Burnt Offerings—Read "Comment" on Lev. 1:2-3 (89-90).

1. Why was it important that an animal given as an offering be "without blemish"?

2. Why was the offering presented at the tent of meeting entrance?

C. Atonement—Read "Comment" on Lev. 1:4-5 (90-91).

1. Why was the offeror instructed to lay their hands on the animal's head?

2. What two main ideas are conveyed by "atonement," and what did each accomplish for the person offering a sacrifice?

3. Which portion of the sacrifice was central to making atonement for the offeror?

D. Jesus as the Final and Ultimate Burnt Offering—Read "Introduction," section 5.f (72).
1. Since the book of Hebrews makes it clear that animal sacrifices were not sufficient to "take away sins" (Heb. 10:4), why did the Lord accept them as atonement for worshippers' sins during Old Testament times?

2. In what way did the Lord himself "cover the debt of the sinner"?

Read the rest of the "Comment" on Lev. 1:6-17 (92-94).

APPLY

Read "Meaning" (94-95).

A. Cost of Atonement—The burnt offering was the most costly offering a worshipper could bring to the Lord because it was wholly consumed by fire on the altar. Unlike the grain, purification, and reparation offerings, of which the priests ate, and the fellowship offering, of which the priests and the offerors ate, the burnt offering was fully given to the Lord; no one ate any of it. By offering the whole animal to the Lord, the Israelites acknowledged that their sinfulness before a holy God was so great that only a full and costly ransom payment would suffice. This is why Jesus' death on behalf of sinners is described in the language of the burnt offering (Eph 5:2). **Briefly describe one or two practical implications for our personal devotion to the Lord and for corporate worship today.**

B. Wholehearted Worship—By giving the Lord the whole animal as a burnt offering, the Israelites also emphasized two things about their accompanying prayers. Sometimes they emphasized the *seriousness* of their prayers, acknowledging their total dependence on the Lord's help. Other times, they emphasized their *praise and thanksgiving*, acknowledging the Lord's worthiness of all praise and glory. **Describe one or two ways these aspects should affect our prayers to the Lord today.**

RESPOND

Meditate—This week, contemplate the reality that God wants to meet with you—not just corporately on Sundays or during a small group—but also just with you. He wants to spend time with you, listen to you, speak with you, and instruct you in his ways (Ps 25). Meditate on what it cost God the Father to offer his own Son as the final and perfect sacrifice for our sins (Heb 9-10). Consider how you might pattern your prayers to reflect those things the Israelite worshippers acknowledged as they presented their burnt offerings.

Take Action—In light of what you've learned in this lesson about burnt offerings, consider some ways you might offer yourself to the Lord wholeheartedly as a "living sacrifice," holy and pleasing to him as your spiritual act of worship (see Rom 12:1). Go back through the lesson and your notes for ideas. Write down a few concrete steps you might take.

THE BURNT OFFERING

ANALYZE

Opening Prayer

Heavenly Father, as we study your word in Leviticus, which you gave through your servant Moses with whom you met face-to-face as a friend, teach us through the Holy Spirit about right worship, and what your instructions to ancient Israel mean for us and the community with whom we worship. In Jesus' name we pray and give you thanks. Amen.

Share Reflections | 5 min.

Have each person share one reflection from the Reflect exercise on the first page of the Individual Study. You can do this in pairs, or in the larger group if you have time. This is not a time to critique or ask lots of questions of each other, but simply to share something God has put on your heart.

Clarify Issues from the Lesson | 10 min.

Back in the larger group, prepare for your discussion by clarifying any uncertainties about the Scripture or commentary, but be careful with your time. The purpose here is to focus on a few issues that may be particularly difficult, not to open a broad discussion about the lesson.

Meaning of Leviticus for Today | 20 min.

Take turns reading aloud each point below, and discuss the questions as a group:

A. The Tent of Meeting and God's Laws—The Lord called Moses to the tent of meeting and spoke with him to give Israel his laws for worshipping him properly. He intended his laws to help the Israelites live as faithful members of the covenant kingdom in two ways. First, they showed the Israelites how to maintain covenant fellowship with their King, now dwelling in their midst. Second, they showed the Israelites how to reflect his holiness so they could fulfill their covenant mission to be a "kingdom of priests and a holy nation" to "all the earth" (Exod 19:4-6). **Discuss three or four concrete ways these two purposes of God's law should impact our individual <u>and</u> corporate lives of faithfulness and holiness today:**

B. Costly Atonement of Jesus—The burnt offering was the most costly offering because the meat was entirely consumed by fire on the altar (Lev. 1:9, 13, 15). Neither the priests nor the offerors ate any part of it. It was given wholly to the Lord except for anything removed as filth (Lev. 1:16). The Israelites thereby acknowledged that their sinfulness against a holy God was so great that only a costly and complete sacrifice could ransom them from the Lord's judgment (94). **Discuss some concrete ways in which the costliness of God's offering his only Son for our forgiveness and redemption should impact both our personal devotion and corporate worship today:**

- Personal devotion

- Corporate worship

EVALUATE

Whole-hearted Worship | 20 min.

By offering the whole animal as a burnt offering, Israelite worshippers acknowledged their whole or complete dependence on the Lord for atonement, and his worthiness of their complete praise and all glory (94-95). **Evaluate ways your church community and/or small group might excel in whole-hearted worship of the Lord according to the principles you've learned from Leviticus 1. Write down a few steps you might take individually and corporately, to move in this direction:**

LEVITICUS 2

THE GRAIN OFFERING

ENGAGE

Reflect

To be "remembered" by the Lord, according to Scripture, means to receive his favor and care as a worshipper who is keeping covenant with him—that is, walking rightly before him. As you go about your day, do you realize the Lord "remembers" you? Are you aware he cares for you? Do you feel you have his favor in your life? Reflect on these things, and journal your thoughts below.

Pray

Heavenly Father, as I study your word in Leviticus, help me to know you remember me with your care and favor. I pray that by your Holy Spirit, you would convict me and lead me to repent of any ways in which I'm not keeping covenant with you so that I may know your care and favor in my life. In Jesus' name I pray and give you thanks. Amen.

Read

- Read Leviticus 2, which concerns the grain offering. Keep in mind it often accompanied the burnt offering and thus often had the same purpose, which was to provide atonement for the worshipper. See "Context" chart (88).
- In the commentary, read "Introduction," sections 4.a (37-38), 4.c (40-41), and "Context" (95).
- Read Leviticus 2 again.

A. Grain Offerings in General—Review "Context" (95), and read "Comment" on Lev. 2:1-3 (95-97).

1. Why might the Israelites have made grain offerings along with their burnt offerings?

2. What were the three types of grain offerings?

3. What were the ingredients used?

4. What was likely the significance of the "fine flour"?

5. What did the frankincense and its costliness acknowledge in the uncooked grain offering?

B. Portions of the Grain Offering—Read "Comment" on Lev. 2:2-3 (97-98).

1. What were the two portions of the grain offering called?

2. Which portion was burned on the altar as a food offering, a pleasing aroma to the Lord?

3. Which of the portions included frankincense, and why (see bottom of 96)?

4. What was the purpose of the priests' portion?

C. Significance of the Memorial Portion—Review "Comment" on Lev. 2:2-3 (97). The memorial portion of the grain offering served not only as a token of the offering itself but also to bring the offeror to the Lord's "remembrance". This did not mean, however, that the Lord had forgotten the offeror.

1. What, then, did it mean for an Israelite worshipper to be "remembered" before the Lord?

2. What are specific examples of ways the Lord might "remember" Israelite worshippers in connection with their petitions?

3. How did the thief who died next to Jesus seek "remembrance" from the Lord (see Lk. 23:42)?

D. Salt in the Grain Offering—Read "Comment" on Lev. 2:13 (100). Lev. 2:13 calls the salt that was to be included in all grain offerings, indeed in all offerings, the "salt of the covenant with your God."

  1. What was the covenant in view here?

  2. What kind of affirmation in worship did the salt of the offerings serve?

Read the rest of the "Comment" on Lev. 2:4-12, and 14-16 (98-100).

APPLY

A. Providing for the Priesthood—Review "Comment" on Lev. 2:2-3 (97). Also read Neh. 13:10-12 and 1 Cor. 9:13-14. As part of the Israelite's various tithes to the Lord, he assigned portions of the offerings to the priests to be eaten by them as their share of the food offerings (Lev. 27:30-32; Num. 18:24). This served to remind the priests that the Lord was their inheritance or "portion," since the priestly tribe of Levi would not receive an inheritance of land in Canaan as the other tribes would (Josh. 13:14, 33; see also Josh. 14:4). If the Israelite worshippers failed to bring sufficient offerings to provide for the priests, the priests would be forced to leave their ministry in the tabernacle in order to provide food for themselves, and the worship of the Lord would suffer. **What are some implications of this for us today as we bring our monetary offerings of finances to the Lord, as well as our gifts of service?**

B. Salt of the Covenant—Read "Meaning" (100-101). In the context of ancient covenants, salt signified a covenant's permanence. Thus in Israel, the "salt of the covenant" signified the permanence of the covenant the Lord made with Israel at Mt. Sinai after delivering her from Egypt. By requiring the Israelites to add salt to their offerings, the Lord provided a way for them to continually affirm their covenant relationship with him. This would have greatly encouraged the people, reminding them of his steadfast commitment to be their covenant King.

1. Read Mt 26:26-29. How has the Lord signified the permanence of his covenant for believers today and provided a way for us to affirm our covenant relationship with him?

2. The salt of the covenant reminded the Israelites of their covenant King's presence in their midst, giving them confidence to pursue their mission of reflecting his holy character to the world (101). Read Mt. 28:18-20. How should the promise of Jesus' presence impact the way we live our lives among non-believing neighbors, family, friends, and others in our circles of influence?

RESPOND

Meditate—Meditate this week on the reality that the Lord remembers you in your praise and petitions, that you have his favor and that he cares for you according to his sovereign wisdom. Meditate on Psalm 25, especially verses 6-7: "Remember your mercy, O Lord, and your steadfast love, for they have been from old. Remember not the sins of my youth or my transgressions. According to your steadfast love remember me, for the sake of your goodness, O Lord."

Take Action—Consider what you are learning about how our covenant obligations to the Lord inform how we witness the Gospel to our neighbors and community, namely, that we are to reflect the character of our King by keeping his commands. Are there any social interactions in your life—at work, in your neighborhood, in your children's school, in a community organization, *etc.*—where you might excel all the more in your covenant faithfulness to the Lord and so more perfectly reflect his character to others? Make a short, practical plan for effecting those changes.

THE GRAIN OFFERING

ANALYZE

Opening Prayer

Heavenly Father, as we study your word in Leviticus, help us to know that you remember us with your care and favor. We pray that by your Holy Spirit you would convict us and lead us to repent of any ways in which we are not keeping covenant with you, so that we may know your care and favor in our lives. In Jesus' name we pray and give you thanks. Amen.

Share Reflections | 5 min.

Have each person share one reflection from the Reflect exercise on the first page of the Individual Study. You can do this in pairs, or in the larger group if you have time. This is not a time to critique or ask lots of questions of each other, but simply to share something God has put on your heart.

Clarify Issues from the Lesson | 10 min.

Back in the larger group, prepare for your discussion by clarifying any uncertainties about the Scripture or commentary, but be careful with your time. The purpose here is to focus on a few issues that may be particularly difficult, not to open a broad discussion about the lesson.

Meaning of Leviticus for Today | 20 min.

Take turns reading aloud each point below, and discuss the questions as a group:

A. The Lord's Remembrance—The memorial portion of the grain offering served to bring offerors to the Lord's "remembrance" as they presented their praise and petitions before him. To be "remembered" by the Lord meant to receive his favor and care. The thief who died with Jesus sought the Lord's care and favor when he asked Jesus to "remember" him when he came into his kingdom, which Jesus did (see Lk. 23:42). **How does knowing the Lord remembers us as his people help us as we respond to his calling on our lives to present ourselves to him as "living sacrifices, holy and pleasing to God, as our spiritual act of worship" (Rom. 12:1)?**

B. Providing for the Ministry of God's People—The Lord assigned to the priests portions of the grain and other offerings the Israelites tithed to him to be their share of food (see Lev. 27:32; Num. 18:24). This served to remind the priests that *the Lord* was their inheritance or "portion," since the priestly tribe of Levi did not receive an inheritance of land in Canaan as the other tribes did (see Josh. 13:14, 33). Nehemiah 13:10-12 illustrates a serious and practical implication of the Israelites failing to bring sufficient offerings and tithes to provide for the priests: The priests were forced to leave their ministry in the temple to provide food for themselves and their families from the common pastures and fields (cf., Josh. 14:4).

1. Paul in 1 Cor. 9:13-14 applies the requirement of the priests' portion to the New Testament age when he says, "In the same way, the Lord commanded that those who proclaim the gospel should get their living by the gospel." What does Paul mean?

2. What are some implications of this for the local church in managing its ministries?

C. "Saltiness" of Worship and Witness—By requiring worshippers to add the "salt of the covenant" to their offerings, the Lord provided the Israelites an opportunity to affirm their covenant relationship. This reminded them of his steadfast commitment to be their covenant King. In the same way, Jesus assured us of his covenant presence and authority when he commissioned us to make disciples of all nations (Mt. 28:18-20). The salt also reminded Israel of its covenant obligation to live among the nations as "a kingdom of priests and a holy nation," so they might witness to the Lord's wisdom, righteousness, and holiness (Exod 19:6; Lev. 20:24b-26; Dt. 4:5-9). To follow the King's commands is to reflect his character.

1. Discuss several ways a church might structure and pursue community that affirms its members' covenant relationship with the Lord—especially his steadfast presence with them:

2. Notice that the idea of our witnessing to the world as "a kingdom of priests and a holy nation" is fundamentally about keeping covenant with the Lord. What are some implications of this for the way we pursue evangelism?

3. What might it look like for Christian churches to be "a holy nation" in their communities and "priests" who intercede with the Lord for their communities?

CREATE

Adding Salt to Ministry | 20 min.

Question C, above, concerns the "salt of the covenant" in our worship and witness. Think about your church's ministries, both to its members and in outreach to the community and the world. Are there any areas in which these ministries might further add "the salt of the covenant?" Brainstorm ideas, and write down some practical steps you can take as a small group to bring these ideas to the ministries.

THE FELLOWSHIP OFFERING

ENGAGE

Reflect

When you have special guests for dinner in your home, how do you want them to feel about their relationship with you and importance to you? What things do you do in planning, preparing, serving, and engaging with them during the meal that reflect these desires? In what ways do you take the same care in your daily life to celebrate your relationship with the Lord and honor his importance to you? Reflect on these things, and journal your thoughts below.

Pray

Heavenly Father, as I study your word in Leviticus, help me to know your desire to have fellowship with those who worship you. Help me understand more deeply how we might better acknowledge your fellowship with us in our homes, your sovereignty over our lives, and the honor you are due for your redemption, which has brought us into your covenant community. In Jesus' name I pray and give you thanks. Amen.

Read

- Read Leviticus 3, which concerns the fellowship offering. Keep in mind the fellowship offering was meant to underscore the offeror's covenant relationship with the Lord and other Israelites. See "Context" chart (88).
- In the commentary, read "Introduction" sections 4.g.iv (53-54), 5.e (71-72), and "Context" (101-102).
- Read Leviticus 3 again.

A. Function of Fellowship Offerings—Review "Comment," first paragraph (102): The fellowship and burnt offerings were similar. In each, the offeror brought an unblemished animal to the tent of meeting and laid their hands on the animal's head, after which it was killed, its blood thrown on the altar by the priest and the sacrificial portion of its meat burned in offering to the Lord.

1. What is the key *difference* between these two offerings?

2. What part of the animal was burned on the altar in a fellowship offering?

3. What happened to the rest of the animal?

4. Who were the parties that consumed the offering?

5. What function of the fellowship offering do these differences highlight?

B. Atonement in the Fellowship Offering—Read Lev 3:2, 8, 13; and "Comment" on Lev. 3:2 (102).

1. Though the fellowship offering does not explicitly focus on atonement, why is it apparent from Lev. 3 that atonement was still taking place during this offering?

2. Why shouldn't this surprise us?

C. The Fat of the Fellowship Offering—Read "Comment" on Lev. 3:3-5 (102-104).

1. Why was all the fat of a fellowship offering burned?

2. How did Israelites think of "fat" differently than we moderns may think of it?

3. So what portion of the sacrificial animal or "meal" were the Israelites giving to the Lord, and what did that acknowledge?

D. Significance of Shared Meals—Read "Comment" on Lev. 3:6-15 (104-105). In ancient Israel and other places in the Near East, a meal was to be shared with guests as a sign of hospitality, as it is today. But a shared meal also often signified much more.

1. What purpose could a shared meal serve when the guest was given the very best food?

2. As applied to the fellowship offering, what function did it serve?

3. What other important purpose could a shared meal serve in ancient Israel in terms of the relationship among those eating?

4. As applied to the fellowship offering, what function did it serve?

E. Prohibition Against Consuming Fat or Blood—Read "Comment" on Lev. 3:16-17 (105-106), and Lev. 17:11 (220-222). As we've seen, the Israelites were prohibited from eating the fat of the fellowship offering, which was to be given to the Lord as the very best part and burned on the altar. They were also prohibited from eating blood—that is, raw meat with blood still in it.

1. What was a key reason for this prohibition?

2. What did the Israelites acknowledge by abstaining from raw meat?

3. The prohibition against consuming fat or blood applied not only to animals offered at the tent of meeting, or tabernacle, but also to those eaten at home, whether sacrificial animals or not (see Lev. 3:17). What two things did an Israelite family acknowledge by not eating the fat of the meat, or raw meat with the blood still in it?

APPLY

A. Shared Meals and the Covenant—Read "Meaning" (106-107). As we have seen, Israelites often confirmed a covenant relationship by sharing a meal with other parties to the covenant. Thus the fellowship offering, which was shared among offerors, priests (Lev. 7:28-35), and the Lord, confirmed the covenant between the Lord and Israel, both as a *celebration* and *rededication*: The Israelites celebrated their covenant relationship with the Lord and rededicated themselves to their covenant responsibilities. The fellowship offering was typically eaten with one's household and other members of the covenant community, reminding the Israelites that they belonged to a covenant family (107). **What are some concrete ways a church or Christian fellowship group might eat meals together to celebrate their relationship with the Lord and rededicate themselves to reflecting his holiness to the surrounding world?**

B. Celebrating the Lord's Supper as a Fellowship Meal—Review "Meaning" (107). Jesus used the concept of a shared covenant meal when he instituted the Lord's Supper for members of the new covenant (cf. Lk 22:20 with Exod 24:8). **What are some concrete ways Christian churches might structure their communities' participation in the Lord's Supper to emphasize both celebrating our relationship with him and rededicating ourselves to reflecting his holiness?**

Meditate—Meditate this week on Jesus' words and prayers as he celebrated the Lord's Supper with his disciples. Read John 15 and 17, taking time to reflect on what Jesus is saying, especially how his words in John 15 lead us to *rededicate* ourselves to him as our covenant Lord and to our covenant brothers and sisters, and how his prayer in John 17 leads us to celebrate the redemption he has won for us.

Take Action—As you think about the two purposes of the fellowship offering in Israel (106-107), how might you reflect them in your relationship with the Lord? What are some practical ways you might celebrate his redeeming presence in your life and affirm your covenant relationship with him—both in corporate worship and in your personal walk? Write down a simple plan for implementing your ideas, and start it this week as you meditate on the Lord's desire to have fellowship with his people.

<table>
<tr><td>LEVITICUS 3</td></tr>
</table>

THE FELLOWSHIP OFFERING

ANALYZE

Opening Prayer

Heavenly Father, as we study your word in Leviticus, help us to know your desire to have fellowship with those who worship you. Help us understand more deeply how we might better acknowledge your fellowship with us in our homes, your sovereignty over our lives, and the honor you are due for your redemption, which has brought us into your covenant community. In Jesus' name we pray and give you thanks. Amen.

Share Reflections | 5 min.

Have each person share one reflection from the Reflect exercise on the first page of the Individual Study. You can do this in pairs, or in the larger group if you have time. This is not a time to critique or ask lots of questions of each other, but simply to share something God has put on your heart.

Clarify Issues from the Lesson | 10 min.

Back in the larger group, prepare for your discussion by clarifying any uncertainties about the Scripture or commentary, but be careful with your time. The purpose here is to focus on a few issues that may be particularly difficult, not to open a broad discussion about the lesson.

Meaning of Leviticus for Today | 20 min.

Take turns reading aloud each point below, and discuss the questions as a group:

A. Acknowledging the Lord's Worthiness and Sovereignty—Israelites were forbidden from eating fat and from eating meat with the blood still in it (Lev. 3:17). They were forbidden from eating fat, which was the choicest part of the meat and meal; it was to be given to the Lord as a way of showing he is worthy of all honor and praise (Lev. 3:16; "Comment" [103, 105]). They were forbidden from eating an animal's blood because it was equated with its life and thus belonged to the Lord, who is sovereign over all life. He permitted the Israelites to atone for their sins by using the animals' blood in sacrifice, but they were not to eat the blood as though it belonged to them. See 4.g.iv (53-54); "Comment" (106; 220-222). We no longer follow the Old Testament laws of sacrifice because Jesus became the final sacrifice for sin. See Lesson 1; Heb. 9-10. Still, we are to offer ourselves as living sacrifices to the Lord as our spiritual act of worship (Rom. 12:1). **How should acknowledging the Lord's <u>worthiness</u> and <u>sovereignty</u>, which was signified by the fat and blood of the fellowship offerings, impact the ways in which we offer ourselves to him as living sacrifices?**

B. Experiencing the Lord's Supper—Jesus used the concept of a shared covenant meal when he instituted the Lord's Supper (cf. Lk. 22:20 with Ex. 24:8). It serves the same purposes for members of the new covenant community as the fellowship offering did for Israel: an opportunity to celebrate and honor the worth and sovereignty of our covenant King and to *rededicate* ourselves to his covenant commands to living holy lives and loving and caring for others in the covenant community (106-107).

1. What are some ways a church's celebration of communion might provide an opportunity in word or deed to (a) celebrate the Lord, honoring him as our redeeming covenant King, and (b) rededicate ourselves to the new covenant in his blood (Lk. 22:20)—to loving the Lord by keeping his commands (Jn. 14:21) and loving those in the covenant community (Jn. 15:12)?

2. Where and how have you seen churches do this well?

3. How should the purposes of the Lord's Supper, which is a "shared covenant meal," affect how you prepare your heart for the Lord's table?

4. How should the purposes of this "shared covenant meal" impact the ways you relate to others in your church community after you leave the Lord's table?

CREATE

Sharing Meals in Community | 20 min.

Sharing a meal with guests in ancient Israel often signified more than hospitality. Guests could be given special honor by providing them with the very best portions of the food. Shared meals could also affirm a covenant relationship among those partaking (104-105). Though church life does not always need to center around meals, they are a special way to experience fellowship. **Brainstorm ways your small group or other church community meetings might incorporate the significance of Israel's "shared covenant meal," either in gathering for special meals or in other forms of community. Write down some ideas and make a short plan for sharing them with others in your church or implementing them in your own small group gatherings.**

THE PURIFICATION OFFERING

ENGAGE

Reflect

The apostle John says of God the Father, "If we walk in the light, as he is in the light, we have fellowship with one another and the blood of Jesus his Son cleanses us from all sin" (1 Jn. 1:17). How does your heart respond when someone says Jesus has cleansed your sins? In what ways have you believed and experienced God's cleansing of your sins? Reflect on these things in the space below:

Pray

Heavenly Father, as I study your word in Leviticus, I pray you would guide me into a deeper, more intimate knowledge of your forgiveness and grace toward me and the cleansing of my sins by the atoning sacrifice of Jesus. In his name I pray and give you thanks. Amen.

Read

- Read Leviticus 4, which concerns the "purification offering," perhaps called "sin offering" in your Bible. Keep in mind as you read that its purpose was to provide atonement—that is forgiveness—to the worshipper for whom the offering was made. See "Context" chart (88).
- Read in the commentary, "Context" (107-108), and "Introduction," sections 4.e (42-44), 4.g.iii.1 (51-52). You may want to review section 4.g.i (50) on *kipper*, the Hebrew word for "atonement".
- Read Leviticus 4 again.

UNDERSTAND

A. Purification and Sin—Read the first full paragraph on p. 111, which explains why "purification offering" is a better translation than "sin offering." Then review "Context" (107-108).

1. Who was impacted by the defiling effects of sin in the community of Israel?

2. On whom did an Israelite's sin bring defiling dishonor?

3. What did the Lord provide for Israel to remove this defiling dishonor?

B. Sinners and Unintentional Sin—Read "Comment" on Lev. 4 generally, and 4:1-2 (108-110). Leviticus 4 prescribed two different methods for presenting purification offerings for two groups of worshippers who might sin unintentionally.

1. Identify the four categories of Israelites in these two groups:

2. What was the difference in terms of who could officiate these two categories of offerings?

3. Identify the two scenarios that could involve unintentional sinning:

C. Offerings for High Priest and Corporate Israel—Read "Comment" on Lev. 4:3-21 (110-113). The high priest's sins had serious consequences for the entire community because of his elevated status as the most important minister of worship for Israel.

1. Describe one critical consequence of the high priest's sins in terms of the Lord's response, and give two examples:

2. How could the entire community of Israel sin unintentionally? Give an example:

3. How would Israel learn about its sin?

4. What would this prompt the community to do?

Read the rest of the "Comment" on Lev. 4:22-35 (114).

─────────────────────────── **APPLY** ───────────────────────────

A. Consequences of a Leader's Sin—Read "Meaning" (118). As we've seen, the sins of the high priest, like the sins of all those in authority, were considered more serious because leaders have the greatest potential to lead others astray (see 1 Kgs 12:28-33; 14:16) and to bring dishonor on the Lord's name (2 Sam 12:14). Because the Lord knows that sheep follow the shepherd, he continually emphasizes the need for shepherds to be "examples to the flock" (1 Tim 3:1-13; 4:12; Jas 3:1; 1 Pet 5:3). **Describe two examples of consequences that might result from the sins of church leaders today:**

B. The Defiling Dishonor of Sin—Review "Context" (108) and "Meaning" (118). The Israelites understood that the defilement of sin was like dishonor, which could be brought not only on the sinner but also on his family, on the covenant community, and especially on the Lord's holy dwelling, the tent of meeting. **Give one or two examples of how our sin might bring dishonor on our families or church community?**

C. Defiling God's Holy Temple—The apostle Paul makes it clear that we are the holy "temple," the dwelling place of God, in the New Testament age (1 Cor. 3:16-17; 6:19). **Write one reflection on how this truth should affect the way we think about and deal with our sin:**

D. The Lord's Great Mercy—Review "Meaning" (118). The Lord's purity made it impossible for him to allow his dwelling place to be defiled. But not only is the Lord pure—he is also *merciful*. His great mercy compelled him to provide a way for his people to deal with their defilement: the *purification offering*. Read Titus 2:11-14; and Heb. 1:3-4; 10:10-14. **According to Paul and the writer of Hebrews, how has the Lord in the New Testament age carried his mercy, once exemplified in the purification offering, to completion?**

Meditate—Meditate this week on God's great mercy and grace toward you in the cleansing blood of Jesus, which he gave for you and his Church. Do this by reading and reflecting each day on these truths of Scripture: Jesus' words in Mt. 26:27-28 as he shared the cup with his disciples at his last supper, saying, "This is my blood of the covenant, which is poured out for many for the forgiveness of sins," and Paul's encouragement in Eph. 1:7 that "in Christ we have redemption through his blood, the forgiveness of our sins, according to the riches of his grace…"

Take Action—As you become aware of sin in your life this week, or as any past sins come to mind, take a few notes on your emotional and mental responses. How fully are you able to experience and express thanks for the Lord's forgiveness and cleansing of your sin through Jesus' blood? How free do you feel from the burden of those forgiven sins? Write a few practical steps you can take to begin encouraging your heart and mind that "as far as the east is from the west, so far has the Lord removed your sins" from you (Ps. 103:12). For example, you might print out cards with the Scripture passages above (Mt. 26:27-28; Eph. 1:7) and place them around your home as reminders of God's forgiveness and love for you. You might incorporate them into your prayers this week. You might meet with a friend and talk through your responses to your sin and God's forgiveness, asking them to pray with you for further freedom and knowledge of the cleansing you have received in Jesus.

THE PURIFICATION OFFERING

ANALYZE

Opening Prayer

Heavenly Father, as we study your word in Leviticus, we pray that you would guide us into a deeper, more intimate knowledge of your forgiveness and grace toward each of us and the cleansing of our sins by the atoning sacrifice of Jesus. In his name we pray and give you thanks. Amen.

Share Reflections | 5 min.

Have each person share one reflection from the Reflect exercise on the first page of the Individual Study. You can do this in pairs, or in the larger group if you have time. This is not a time to critique or ask lots of questions of each other, but simply to share something God has put on your heart.

Clarify Issues from the Lesson | 10 min.

Back in the larger group, prepare for your discussion by clarifying any uncertainties about the Scripture or commentary, but be careful with your time. The purpose here is to focus on a few issues that may be particularly difficult, not to open a broad discussion about the lesson.

Meaning of Leviticus for Today | 20 min.

Take turns reading aloud each point below, and discuss the questions as a group:

A. Sins of the Church's Leaders—The Old Testament law considered the sins of the high priest to be of greater consequence than those of ordinary Israelites. The law of the purification offering highlights this by making it clear that the high priest's sins brought guilt on the entire community (Lev. 4:3) and by providing a more elevated form of presenting the offering for the high priest than for ordinary citizens (109-111). This underscores the Lord's view that the sin of those in authority is more serious than the sin of those who are under them, because leaders have the greater potential to lead others astray and to bring dishonor on the Lord (118). The Lord's grace and mercy are sufficient to provide forgiveness and restoration to the leaders and their flock, but such sins nonetheless cause great damage to the body of Christ and the name of the Lord.

1. Discuss potential situations in a church where those in authority might lead their congregations or individual members astray or bring dishonor on the Lord:

2. Discuss some practical safeguards against these kinds of leadership sins:

B. Jesus, the Ultimate Offering for Our Purification—God in his great mercy has brought to perfect completion his provision of purification by offering his Son as the ultimate sacrifice for our sin (Rom. 8:3; Heb. 1:3; 13:11-12). Jesus' atoning death is an offering so powerful and final that it cleanses us from all our sins (Heb. 9:28; 10:10, 12, 14). People in every church need the healing grace and mercy of knowing Jesus has forgiven and cleansed them of their sins—past, present and future. **Share examples of ministries you have experienced, in your church or elsewhere, that have done this well and describe what they did:**

CREATE

Healing through Purification | 20 min.

The final discussion question above concerns the ministry of healing that comes through knowing and experiencing the forgiveness and cleansing of sin by the grace and atoning sacrifice of Christ. **Brainstorm ideas for how ministries in your church might bring even more "healing through purification" to those who need it.** Write down a few practical steps your small group could take to help initiate and facilitate one or more of your ideas.

THE PURIFICATION OFFERING—PART 2

ENGAGE

Reflect

How do you feel when someone apologizes for treating you wrongly, then continues to do so? Think about people in your life who may have done this. Why does their behavior hurt you? Now consider whether you are treating anyone this way. In what ways might this be harming your relationship with them?

Pray

Heavenly Father, as I study your word in Leviticus, I pray you would make me aware through your Holy Spirit of any wrongful ways in my life that I need to confess to you, and help me truly repent of those ways and not turn back to them. In Jesus' name I pray and give you thanks. Amen.

Read

- Read Leviticus 5:1-13, which concerns several specific sins that call for the "purification offering" (perhaps called "sin offering" in your Bible). Keep in mind as you read that the purpose of this offering was to provide atonement—that is, forgiveness—to the worshipper for whom it was made. See "Context" chart (88).
- Read in the commentary, "Context" (107-108), and "Introduction" sections 4.e.i.3 (43-44), 4.g.iii.1 (51-52). You may want to review section 4.g.i (50) on *kipper*, the Hebrew word for "atonement".
- Read Leviticus 5:1-13 again.

A. Purification for Specific Sins—Read "Comment" on Lev. 5:1-13 generally and 5:1-4 (114-116). Leviticus 5:1-13 identifies three specific sins that require a purification offering. Two were *unintentional* sins, which are the primary focus of Lev. 4. One was an *intentional* sin.

1. Describe the two unintentional sins and the one intentional sin, of Lev. 5:1-13:

2. Why was failing to testify in a criminal proceeding considered a serious sin?

3. What was the effect of becoming ritually impure in terms of participating in worship?

4. Although becoming ritually impure normally was not a sin in Israel, why was failing to address the impurity a sin?

5. What were two ways Israelites' impurity or uncleanness might have been "hidden" from them (Lev. 5:2, 3) so that the sin was unintentional?

6. When Israelites swore an oath, they invoked the name of the Lord, asking him to bring judgment on them if they were lying or failed to keep a promise. Why was failing to keep an oath considered a sin requiring a purification offering?

B. Confessing Sin—Read "Comment" on Lev. 5:5-6 (116-117). Leviticus 5:5 makes clear that worshippers were to confess their sins as a condition of receiving atonement through the purification offering. What are the two essential elements of biblical confession?

C. Purification Offerings of Birds and Fine Flour—Read "Comment" on Lev. 5:7-13 (117): The law of Lev. 5:7-10 allowed worshippers to make a purification offering of certain birds or fine flour instead of a female animal from the flock.

1. Who was permitted to bring these purification offerings?

2. What was the Lord's intention in making this gracious provision?

3. What was especially unique about the purification offering of fine flour?

A. Protecting the Poor and Powerless—Review "Comment" on Lev. 5:1 (115). The Lord repeatedly commands his people not to "oppress the widow, the fatherless, the sojourner, or the poor" in social or legal matters but to "defend the orphan [and] plead for the widow" (Zech 7:9–10; Isa 1:17; see also Exod 23:6–7; Deut 27:19; Prov 22:22; Isa 1:23). **How might the ethical values embodied in the law of Lev. 5:1 be relevant to this repeated admonition from the Lord for social and legal justice?**

B. Dealing with Our Impurity—Review "Comment" on Lev. 5:2-3 (115-116). Though becoming ritually impure was not normally a sin for Israelites, failing properly address it was a serious matter (Lev. 5:2-3) because they risked committing the very serious sin of defiling the Lord's dwelling place, the tabernacle (Lev. 15:31). **How does the New Testament, in Paul's admonition in 1 Cor. 6:18-20, reflect the Lord's concern that his holy dwelling place not be defiled?**

C. Confessing and Righting our Wrongs—Review "Comment" on Lev. 5:5-6 (116-117). Forgiveness for the Israelites meant acknowledging their wrongdoings and correcting them wherever possible: Confession had to be genuine, not just words. **How does the New Testament, in the apostle John's words in 1 Jn. 1:6-9, reflect this principle?**

RESPOND

Meditate—The Old Testament laws concerning *ritual* purity pointed to the spiritual reality that the Lord desires moral purity in those who worship him. David sang of this reality in Ps. 51, when he petitioned the Lord, "cleanse me of my sin" (v. 2), and "create in me a clean heart" (v. 10). David recognized the Lord did not delight in the Israelites' sacrifices in themselves (v. 16) but desires the true spiritual sacrifice of "a broken spirit, a broken and contrite heart" (17). Meditate on Ps. 51 this week, and make it your prayer to the Lord.

Take Action—Choose someone you identified in your reflection at the beginning of this lesson that you perhaps continue to treat wrongly, though you've acknowledged the wrong. Write down a few practical steps you can take to make a genuine confession to them and stop treating them wrongly. Begin taking some of those steps this week.

THE PURIFICATION OFFERING—PART 2

ANALYZE

Opening Prayer

Heavenly Father, as we study your word in Leviticus, we pray you would make us aware through your Holy Spirit of any wrongful ways in our individual lives and our life as a church that we need to confess to you, and help us to repent permanently of those ways. In Jesus' name we pray and give you thanks. Amen.

Share Reflections | 5 min.

Have each person share one reflection from the Reflect exercise on the first page of the Individual Study. You can do this in pairs, or in the larger group if you have time. This is not a time to critique or ask lots of questions of each other, but simply to share something God has put on your heart.

Clarify Issues from the Lesson | 10 min.

Back in the larger group, prepare for your discussion by clarifying any uncertainties about the Scripture or commentary, but be careful with your time. The purpose here is to focus on a few issues that may be particularly difficult, not to open a broad discussion about the lesson.

Meaning of Leviticus for Today | 20 min.

Take turns reading aloud each point below, and discuss the questions as a group:

A. Speaking for the Powerless—Lev. 5:1 concerns the sin of failing to testify in a legal proceeding. This sin bore directly on the Lord's repeated commands not to "oppress the widow, the fatherless, the sojourner, or the poor" in legal or social matters, but to "defend the orphan [and] plead for the widow" (Zech. 7:9–10; Isa. 1:17; see also Ex. 23:6–7; Dt. 27:19; Prov. 22:22; Isa. 1:23). **Discuss three or four situations in our contemporary society where the Church's failure to speak on behalf of those who lack relative political or legal power may amount to the sin of Lev. 5:1.**

B. Confessing and Righting our Wrongs—Forgiveness for the Israelites meant acknowledging their wrongdoings and correcting them wherever possible: Confession had to be genuine, not just words. The New Testament reflects this same principle. The apostle John makes this clear in 1 Jn. 1:6-9, where he says, "If we say we have fellowship with God while we walk in darkness, we lie and do not practice the truth. [But if] we confess our sins, he is faithful and just to forgive us our sins, and cleanse us from all unrighteousness." **Discuss some ways the Church might confess one or more of the sins you identified in question A above and steps it might take to begin "walking in the light" and "practicing truth" in this regard.**

EVALUATE

Equal Access to Worship | 20 min.

The Lord in Lev. 5:7-13 provided for less-wealthy members of the community to bring purification offerings of certain birds or grain preparations instead of more expensive female animals from the flock. Remarkably, the grain offering of fine flour provided atonement to the worshipper even though it did not involve the lifeblood of a sacrificial animal. The Lord in his sovereignty permitted this accommodation to reflect his desire that all people have equal access to worship him, regardless of wealth, power, or status. See "Comment" (117). **Consider whether your own church or churches in your community might be facilitating attitudes, practices, or circumstances that limit or discourage those who are relatively poor or powerless from worshipping the Lord. Write down a few practical steps your church or small group could take to initiate even one small change in this regard.**

THE REPARATION OFFERING

ENGAGE

Reflect

Meditate for a moment on things in this life and world you consider sacred or holy, such as the love between friends or family or the beauty of the mountains in the early morning. Now capture in a few sentences your emotional responses to imagining the violation of these sacred or holy things.

Pray

Heavenly Father, as I study your word in Leviticus, I pray you would increase my sensitivity to the holiness of your Church for which Jesus died, the holiness of my body, which Jesus bought with his death, and the holiness of your name, which I profess to those around me. In Jesus' holy name I pray. Amen.

Read

- Read Leviticus 5:14 – 6:7, which concerns the "reparation offering," translated "guilt offering" in some Bibles. Keep in mind that its purpose was to provide atonement—that is, forgiveness—to worshippers who had committed a breach of faith against the Lord's holy things. It did so by "repairing" or compensating for that breach (Lev. 5:15-16; 6:2, 6-7). See "Context" chart (88).
- In the commentary, review "Introduction", section 4.b (39-40) and read "Context" (118-119).
- Read Leviticus 5:14 – 6:7 again.

UNDERSTAND

A. Breach of Faith Toward the King's Property—Review "Context" (118-119), and read "Comment" on Lev. 5:14-6:7 generally (119) and 5:14-16 (119-122). The reparation offering of Lev. 5:14-6:7 focused on sins that betrayed covenant loyalty, particularly sins of unfaithfulness toward the Lord's *property*. In the ancient Near East, as in most cultures today, disrespecting a person's property meant disrespecting the person.

1. The reparation offering served as an atoning ransom payment for unfaithfulness or "breach of faith" concerning the Lord's "holy things" (Lev. 5:15). This reference to "breach of faith" is strong language that describes treachery in breaking faith with a covenant partner, much like adultery in the marriage relationship (see Num 5:12). Identify four other examples of this strong language of unfaithfulness used in the Old Testament concerning the relationship between Israel and the Lord (120):

2. In Lev. 5: 14-16, "holy things" probably refers to portions of food offerings that were not to be burned on the altar, but instead given to the priests. The Lord had designated these as "most holy" and had given them to the priests and their families (Num. 18:9-14; Lev. 2:10; 6:17, 25-26; 10:12-14). How might an Israelite be unfaithful regarding these particular holy things?

3. Why would unfaithfulness regarding the Lord's "holy things" be considered such a serious sin?

4. In the ancient Near East, how could someone atone for such a breach of covenant loyalty?

B. Reparation and Restitution—Review "Comment" on Lev. 5:15-16 (120-121). A worshipper bringing a reparation offering was to give a ram without blemish to the priests for sacrifice. Worshippers apparently purchased the rams at the tabernacle with silver at the market rate. At that time in Israel, adult male sheep were apparently especially valuable livestock.

1. What did the costliness of the sacrificial ram underscore in the reparation offering?

2. The Hebrew word *asham* for "reparation offering" (often translated "guilt offering") refers elsewhere in the Old Testament to a penalty that must be paid for the consequences of guilt. In the case of the reparation offering, what function did this penalty serve?

3. Before bringing a reparation offering for inadvertently eating some of the holy food offerings, a worshipper first needed to make restitution, replacing the food item and adding a fifth (20 percent), to the value of what had been eaten (Lev. 5:16). To whom would the worshipper make restitution and why?

C. Reparation for an Unknown Sin—Read "Comment" on Lev. 5:17-19 (122-123). This aspect of the reparation offering was apparently intended to provide forgiveness to those inadvertently unfaithful in something *of which they never become aware* (such as unknowingly eating food meant only for the priests and their families). This may explain why restitution is not mentioned here, as it is in verses 14-16, since the sinner would never know what to repay. This section also apparently concerns a breach of faith toward the Lord's holy things, since the texts immediately before (5:14-16) and after (6:1-7) deal with that subject.

1. How would an Israelite worshipper know to bring a reparation offering in such case?

2. Note that suffering was not then—and is not now—necessarily a sign the sufferer had sinned. The story of Job makes this clear, as does Jesus' teaching that the blind man's condition was not the result of his or his parents' sin (Jn. 9:1-3). If a worshipper continued suffering after a reparation offering, this would assure them before the Lord that their suffering was simply the result of living in a broken world, and their conscience could be clear. If the suffering stopped, however, what might the worshipper reasonably conclude?

D. Reparation for Misusing the Lord's Holy Name—Read "Comment" on Lev. 6:1-7 (123-125). This final aspect of the reparation offering deals with situations in which an Israelite defrauded someone concerning a property right and lied about it by swearing a false oath. This required restitution of the property's value, plus a 20 percent penalty and an offering of a reparation ram to the Lord for atonement.

1. Why would one Israelite defrauding another be considered an act of covenant unfaithfulness against the Lord's holy property?

2. An Israelite would typically maintain their innocence in a matter by taking an oath invoking the name of the Lord as witness and asking that he bring calamity on them if they were guilty (e.g., Num. 5:16-22; 1 Kg. 8:31-32). Why was invoking the Lord's name in swearing a false oath viewed as profaning his holy name?

3. If someone who swore a false oath finally succeeded in defrauding their neighbor, what would prompt them to confess their sin and bring restitution to the wronged party and a reparation offering to the Lord?

APPLY

A. Respecting the Holy Things of the Lord—Read "Meaning" (122). The law of reparation offerings reminded Israelites of the importance of respecting their holy King by respecting his holy property, namely, the holy food offerings for the priests and the Lord's holy name. The New Testament carries forward this concern for respecting God's "holy things" in many areas of Christian life. In 1 Cor. 6:12-20, Paul warns that sexual immorality is a sin against our own bodies, reminding us that our bodies are "the temple of the Holy Spirit" and no longer belong to us, but were bought with a price by the sacrifice of Jesus (1 Cor. 6:19-20). "So," says Paul, "glorify God in your bodies." Paul also warns in 1 Cor. 3:16-17 against harming God's people, since they make up his holy temple.

1. Describe (a) one way we might glorify God with our bodies (1 Cor 6:12-20) and (b) one way we can harm God's holy temple, his people the Church (1 Cor 3:16-17)?

2. In 2 Thess. 1:11-12, Paul writes, "With this in mind, we constantly pray for you, that our God may make you worthy of his calling, and that by his power he may bring to fruition your every desire for goodness and your every deed prompted by faith. We pray this so that the name of our Lord Jesus may be glorified in you…" Identify two or three "desires for goodness" or "deeds prompted by faith" you might pursue by God's power to glorify Jesus' name, and describe how they would glorify his name:

RESPOND

Meditate—Before Israelite worshippers could bring a reparation offering to the Lord for forgiveness, they had to make restitution to members of the community against whom they had sinned (Lev 5:16; 6:5). Jesus echoes this command when he says, "Therefore, if you are offering your gift at the altar and there remember that your brother or sister has something against you, leave your gift there in front of the altar. First go and be reconciled to them; then come and offer your gift" (Mt 5:23–24). In other words, Jesus is teaching that God is not interested in our worship if we are unwilling to reconcile with those we have wronged, who are made in his image. Take time this week to meditate on the Lord's words in Mt 5:23-24 and reflect on this truth.

Take Action—As you meditate this week on Jesus' words in Matthew 5, try to identify anyone in your church community or family to whom you need to be reconciled, even in some small way. If you think of someone you have wronged, write down a few practical steps you can take to seek reconciliation, remembering that true reconciliation entails making things right (namely, making restitution), not simply asking for forgiveness. Take the steps you have identified to pursue genuine reconciliation to your brother or sister.

THE REPARATION OFFERING

ANALYZE

Opening Prayer

Heavenly Father, as we study your word in Leviticus, we pray that you would increase our sensitivity to the holiness of your Church for which Jesus died, the holiness of our bodies, which Jesus bought with his death, and the holiness of your name, which we profess to the world around us. In Jesus' holy name we pray. Amen.

Share Reflections | 5 min.

Have each person share one reflection from the Reflect exercise on the first page of the Individual Study. You can do this in pairs, or in the larger group if you have time. This is not a time to critique or ask lots of questions of each other, but simply to share something God has put on your heart.

Clarify Issues from the Lesson | 10 min.

Back in the larger group, prepare for your discussion by clarifying any uncertainties about the Scripture or commentary, but be careful with your time. The purpose here is to focus on a few issues that may be particularly difficult, not to open a broad discussion about the lesson.

Meaning of Leviticus for Today | 20 min.

Take turns reading aloud each point below, and discuss the questions as a group:

A. Respecting the Holy Things of the Lord—The law of the reparation offering reminded Israelites of the importance of respecting their holy King by respecting his holy property. The New Testament carries forward this concern for respecting God's "holy things" in many areas of Christian life (122).

1. In 1 Cor. 3:1-23, Paul warns believers that the church belongs to God as his "holy temple" and that divisions they were creating in the church could "destroy" or damage God's holy temple (1 Cor. 3:16-17). Identify and explain two or three ways believers in a local church can disrespect God's holy temple by causing divisions in the body of Christ:

2. Now describe some practical steps a church's leadership and lay ministers might take to minimize such divisions. Be sure to consider avenues for teaching about the holy things of God that might help in this regard:

B. Dishonoring God's Holy Name—The reparation offering of Lev. 6:1-7 deals with unfaithfulness concerning the Lord's holy name. To profane the name of the Lord entails treating it lightly, using it any way one pleases, rather than as a very holy thing to be deeply respected and invoked with great care (125). The New Testament carries forward this concern for respecting the Lord's name. In Rom. 2:21-24, Paul rebuked the church in Rome for hypocrisy in preaching God's commandments while failing to keep them in their own lives. Then, quoting from Isaiah, Paul says, "The name of God is blasphemed among the Gentiles because of you." He is warning against the dishonor that comes to God's name when those who profess to be Christians fail to live by what they profess. **Identify and explain two or three aspects of the American church's "profession of faith" in which it may be dishonoring God's name in this way:**

EVALUATE

Dishonoring and Glorifying the Lord's Name | 20 min.

As discussed above, the Scriptures show deep concern for treating the Lord's name with utmost respect as his holy possession and that failing to live by what we profess may dishonor his holy name. But God also says that we glorify him when we are "insulted for the name of Christ" (1 Pet. 4:14) and "hated" for his name's sake (Mt. 10:22; Mk. 13:3; Lk. 21:17). **Discuss the distinction between dishonoring God's name and being insulted or hated for his name's sake. Now evaluate whether your own church may be dishonoring God's name in any of its ministries and whether it is being "insulted or hated" for the sake of the Lord's name:**

LEVITICUS 6:8-23

PROPER WORSHIP: BURNT AND GRAIN OFFERINGS

ENGAGE

Reflect

Spend time thinking about any difficult circumstances you may be facing. Write down some of your feelings about those circumstances, then reflect on your feelings about your relationship with God and his concern for you. Pay particular attention to how your prayer life is doing under the circumstances and the extent to which you are continually bringing your need for God's help before him.

Pray

Heavenly Father, as I study your word in Leviticus, I pray that you would bring me to a deeper realization of how much I need to depend upon your grace and mercy in my life and that you would strengthen me to bring this need before you regularly in prayer. In Jesus' name I pray. Amen.

Read

- Read Leviticus 6:8-23, which begins a new section in the book (Lev. 6:8-7:38). This new section comprises instructions primarily to the priests concerning the proper handling of the five major offerings of Lev. 1:1-6:7. In other words, this new section concerns how the priests were to lead Israel (and themselves) in proper worship before the Lord.
- In the commentary, read "Context" (126-127).
- Read Leviticus 6:8-23 again.

A. Commands to the Priests for Proper Worship—Review "Context" (126-127). While the first major section of Leviticus (1:1-6:7) is addressed to lay Israelites (1:2) and describes the general laws of the five major offerings, this next section (6:8-7:38) is addressed primarily to the priests (6:9). It also deals with the five major offerings but differs from the first section in three important ways:

1. First, this section focuses more specifically on *proper handling* of portions of the offerings. Why was proper handling of the offerings so crucial to Israel's worship of the Lord?

2. Second, this section introduces *categories* among the major offerings. Identify three of these categories:

3. Third, this section *orders* the offerings differently than Lev. 1:1-6:7 (see Chart, 127). Describe one possibility for this different organization:

B. Proper Worship and the Continual Fire—Read "Comment" on Lev. 6:8-9a and 6:9b-13 (127-128). As we've seen, this new section in Leviticus deals generally with the priests' proper handling, distribution, and disposal of various portions of the five major offerings. Therefore, for the first time in the book, the Lord tells Moses to address the priests directly (6:9).

1. Why were these laws so vital for the priests?

2. Lev. 6:9b-13 introduces a new category of burnt offering: the *continual burnt offering*. This offering is first described in Ex. 29:38-42. When were the lambs of this offering sacrificed?

3. What do Lev. 6:12a and 13 say about the fire on the altar?

4. The law for the continual burnt offering addressed two practical needs resulting from this kind of offering. Summarize these two practical needs, and how the priests were to meet them:

C. The Laws of the Grain Offering and Continual Grain Offering—Read "Comment" on Lev. 6:14-18 and 6:19-23 (129, 129-130). These next two sections concern the grain offering, which was introduced in Lev. 2:1-16 (see Chart, 127).

1. Leviticus 6:14-18 elaborates on a key aspect of the grain offering that was only briefly mentioned in Lev. 2. Identify that aspect and explain in your own words the rationale behind it:

2. Leviticus 6:19-23 also addresses the grain offering but introduces a new category or type that differs in three ways from the people's grain offering of Lev. 2. Briefly describe these differences:

3. This new category of grain offering was "continual" because the priests were to make the offering daily, once in the morning and once in the evening. Therefore, how did each day in Israel begin and end in terms of the priests' performance of this offering?

A. Worship, Diligence, and the Continual Fire—Read "Meaning" (128). Leviticus 6:8-13 mentions three times that the fire on the altar was to be "kept burning" by the priests (vv. 9b, 12, 13). Since the purpose of the burnt offering was to seek the Lord's favor, the requirement for a continual fire was meant to teach the priests and other Israelites that they were to have a posture of continual dependence and worship before the Lord.

1. Jesus taught his disciples to pray in a posture of continual dependence on God. How is this reflected in the Lord's Prayer (Mt. 6:11; Lk. 11:3)?

2. The New Testament shares the same concern for the "continual fire" of Leviticus, namely, that we continually worship God. Summarize this command as reflected in Eph. 5:20, Phil. 4:4, and 1 Thess. 5:16-18:

3. For the sacrificial fire to burn continually, the priests needed to perform their duties diligently. Otherwise, the right and proper worship of God would suffer. The New Testament reflects this same concern for diligent leadership among God's people. Identify three or four aspects of diligent leadership in Paul's instructions to Timothy in 2 Tim. 2:1-3; 14-15, and 4:1-5:

B. The Priests' Calling to Holiness and Humility—Read "Meaning" (129, 130). The special law of the grain offering (Lev. 6:14-18) was addressed to the priesthood (6:9), implying that the priests themselves were to be careful to treat this offering properly because it was *most holy* to the Lord (Lev. 6:17). Likewise, for the continual grain offering (Lev. 6:19-23), the priests were to carefully make the offering morning and evening, seeking the Lord's favor for the priests themselves.

1. In the command to treat the most holy grain offering with great care, the priests were to see their role as modeling for Israel that the Lord's holiness must always be respected. Identify two or three exhortations by Paul to Timothy in 1 Tim. 4:11-16 that reflect this same concern for New Testament leaders:

2. The priests' twice-daily presentation of the continual grain offering reminded them that though they differed from other Israelites in office and function, they were the same in terms of their need for the Lord and his mercy and grace. This warned them against one of the strongest temptations faced by leaders of God's people: spiritual pride. The apostle Peter addresses the need for humility in church elders and younger members alike in 1 Pet. 5:1-9. Identify three or four behaviors described in that text that apparently go hand-in-hand with remaining humble:

RESPOND

Meditate—Read again, slowly and reflectively, the Lord's commands for the offerings in Lev. 6:8-23. As you read, visualize every action as it would take place. Imagine the sounds and smells that would have filled the air. Imagine how it felt physically, emotionally, and spiritually for the priests to carry out each requirement. Imagine how it felt for the lay Israelites to witness the priests perform a grain offering on their behalf (6:14-18). Imagine how it felt for the high priest to witness the offerings of 6:19-23 being made every day and night, as a constant reminder of the Lord's presence and the need to continually worship him.

Take Action—We are commanded to love the Lord our God with all our heart, soul, strength, and mind—not just with our minds (Lk. 10:27). Sometimes we need visual, aural, tactile, or other physical means to help us express our devotion to God. As you imagine the sights, sounds, smells, and other physical aspects of the worship described in Lev. 6:8-23, consider what you might do in your own home, workplace, and other spaces to create analogous physical prompts or other means to "rejoice always, pray without ceasing, and give thanks in all circumstances" (1 Thess. 5:16-18). Take a few concrete steps to create these physical manifestations of continual worship in your life:

Proper Worship: Burnt and Grain Offerings

ANALYZE

Opening Prayer

Heavenly Father, as we study your word in Leviticus, we pray you would bring us to a deeper realization of how much we need to depend upon your grace and mercy in our lives, and that you would strengthen us to bring this need before you regularly in prayer. In Jesus' name we pray. Amen.

Share Reflections | 5 min.

Have each person share one reflection from the Reflect exercise on the first page of the Individual Study. You can do this in pairs, or in the larger group if you have time. This is not a time to critique or ask lots of questions of each other, but simply to share something God has put on your heart.

Clarify Issues from the Lesson | 10 min.

Back in the larger group, prepare for your discussion by clarifying any uncertainties about the Scripture or commentary, but be careful with your time. The purpose here is to focus on a few issues that may be particularly difficult, not to open a broad discussion about the lesson.

Meaning of Leviticus for Today | 20 min.

Take turns reading aloud each point below, and discuss the questions as a group:

A. Physical Expression of Constant Praise and Prayers—The presence of the continual fire and burnt offerings of Lev. 6:9b-13 on the altar—day and night—was a physical, visual, tactile and aromatic reminder to the Israelites that the holy Lord lived in their midst and was worthy of their constant worship. **Explore some practical ways your church or small group, and you as individuals, can implement more visual, aural, tactile, or other physical reminders or means to continually worship the Lord:**

B. Holiness and Humility in Leaders—The command to the priests in Lev. 6:14-18 to treat the most holy grain offering with great care demonstrated that the priests were to model honoring the Lord's holiness. Likewise, their twice-daily presentation of the continual grain offering (Lev. 6:19-23) reminded them that though they differed from other Israelites in office and function, they were the same in terms of their need for the Lord and his mercy and grace. This warned them against one of the strongest temptations faced by leaders of God's people: spiritual pride.

1. Discuss some practical ways your church community might strategically help your pastors and elders model respect for the Lord's holiness to the entire community:

2. Discuss some practical ways your church community might strategically help your pastors and elders grow in humility and avoid spiritual pride:

CREATE

Faithful Work in Worship | 20 min.

For the sacrificial fire to burn continually (see Lev. 6:9b, 12, 13), the priests needed to perform their duties diligently. Otherwise, the right and proper worship of God would suffer. The New Testament reflects this same concern for faithful leadership among God's people (e.g., 2 Tim. 2:1-3; 14-15, and 4:1-5). **Brainstorm practical steps that members of your church community—perhaps a team from your small group—might commit to helping your pastors, elders, and staff continue performing their ministry duties faithfully and diligently so that your church's worship of God would always be pleasing to him. Make a plan for implementing the steps you determine:**

PROPER WORSHIP: PURIFICATION AND REPARATION OFFERINGS

ENGAGE

Reflect

Write a few brief reflections on *how you think about holiness*. What does "holiness" mean to you? What does it mean to the culture in which you live? How do you think of God's holiness? What do you think about your own holiness? How often during the week do you consider your own holiness? What disciplines do you have in place to guide your personal holiness?

Pray

Heavenly Father, as I study your word in Leviticus, I pray you would create in me a deep desire to honor your holiness by reflecting it in my own life. By the truth of your word and by your Holy Spirit, set me apart from the things that dishonor you. In Jesus' name I pray. Amen.

Read

- Read Lev. 6:24-7:10, which concerns the purification offering, the reparation offering, and the proper distribution of portions of the burnt and grain offerings. By way of reminder, this section comes in the midst of Lev. 6:8-7:38, which deals with the proper handling of the five major offerings, especially by the priests. They needed to ensure this proper handling as a way of treating the Lord with full respect.
- In the commentary, read "Introduction," section 4.f (44-49), and review "Context" (126-127).
- Read Lev. 6:24-7:10 again.

UNDERSTAND

A. Ritual States and the Most Holy Offerings—Lev. 6:24-7:7 concerns the priests' treatment of the "most holy" portions of the purification and reparation offerings (Lev. 6:25, 29; 7:1, 6). To understand why treating the offerings carefully was so important, it is helpful to first understand the concept of "ritual purity". Refer to "Introduction," section 4.f (44-49):

1. Sin and ritual impurity are related ideas in the Old Testament, but they differ in important ways. For example, while sin is rooted in moral wrongdoing, ritual impurity is not. If sin is a *moral action*, then what is impurity?

2. What were the three general "ritual states" in Old Testament Israel?

3. What guidance did these ritual states provide for the community?

4. How might we think of ritual states using the modern analogy of physical health and cleanness?

5. Ritual *purity* was an Israelite's "default" state, but that state could change depending on certain activities or events. Name two means by which one might move from a lower to higher ritual state—that is, from *impurity to purity* or from *purity to holiness*—and two means by which one might move from a higher to lower state—that is, from holiness to purity or from *purity to impurity*:

6. Briefly describe the three purposes of ritual states in Old Testament Israel:

B. Proper Handling of the Most Holy Offerings—Read "Comment" on Lev. 6:24-30 (130-131), and Lev. 7:1-7 (132). This section of Leviticus instructs the high priest Aaron and his sons on specific matters concerning the purification and reparation offerings, most of which focus on their most holy status:

1. Identify the holy place where the purification offering was to be sacrificed.

2. The *purification* offering's "most holy" status meant its meat and blood were to be treated very carefully. What were two requirements for eating this meat after its fat had been removed and burned?

3. The holiness of the sacrificial meat and blood led to regulations for proper handling of other items involved, such as containers and priests' garments. A blood-splattered garment had to be washed in a holy place. Briefly describe two possible reasons:

4. Similarly, a bronze pot used for boiling the sacrifice had to be washed in a holy place, but a clay pot had to be broken. What is the likely reason?

5. Regulations for proper treatment of the *reparation* offering were similar to those of the purification offering. It had to be sacrificed in a holy place and eaten by holy people in a holy place, but its blood was treated differently. How so?

C. Distribution of Offering Portions to the Priests—Read "Comment" on Lev. 7:8-10 (132-133). This section regulates how various portions of the offerings were to be distributed among the priests.

1. Lev. 7:8 provides that the hide of the sacrificial animal should go to the priest who performed the burnt offering. How did this regulation meet a practical need?

2. The regulation for cooked and uncooked grain offerings (Lev. 7:9-10) also met a practical need of the priests. But the cooked grain offering went to the priest making the offering, while the uncooked grain offering belonged to all the priests. Briefly describe one possible reason for this difference:

APPLY

A. Treating the "Living Sacrifices" of Our Lives with Concern for Holiness—Review "Introduction", section 4.f.iv (48-49). The ritual states reinforced Israel's understanding of the Lords' holiness and its calling to reflect his holiness to surrounding cultures by respecting and guarding what he had declared holy. The ritual states also served as a constant reminder to the Israelites that they were to pursue *moral* holiness in all aspects of their lives.

1. Jesus taught this same principle in his earthly ministry. Describe in your own words what he was trying to communicate to the Pharisees in the interaction recorded in Lk. 11:37-41:

2. Give an example of how we in the New Testament church can demonstrate the same error Jesus was pointing out to the Pharisees in the passage above:

3. Give an example of how we might take the same sort of care with the holiness of our "living sacrifices" to God (Rom. 12:1) that the Israelites took with the most holy offerings to the Lord:

RESPOND

Meditate—Meditate this week on David's prayer in Psalm 51. He recognized that God's desire for holiness is focused on the condition of our hearts and "a willing spirit" (Ps. 51:12), not on our rituals of worship. "For you will not delight in sacrifice, or I would give it. You will not be pleased with a burnt offering. The sacrifices of God are a broken sprit—a broken and contrite heart, O God, you will not despise" (Ps. 51:16-17). David knew Israel could worship rightly before the Lord only if the Holy Spirit cleansed their hearts and renewed their spirit. "Then you will delight in right sacrifices, in burnt offerings and whole burnt offerings. Then bulls will be offered on your altar" (Ps. 51:19).

Take Action—As David knew, holiness before the Lord requires the cleansing grace of the Holy Spirit. But Scripture is clear that we are active participants in our sanctification (see, for example, Phil. 2:12-13). In 2 Tim. 2:20-22, Paul uses the analogy that we are "vessels for honorable use, set apart as holy, useful to the master of the house, ready for every good work." Write a few concrete, practical steps you can take to continue being "set apart as holy." Begin taking those steps this week.

PROPER WORSHIP: PURIFICATION AND REPARATION OFFERINGS

ANALYZE

Opening Prayer

Heavenly Father, as we study your word in Leviticus, we pray you would create a deep desire in us to honor your holiness by reflecting it in our own lives. By the truth of your word and by your Holy Spirit, set us apart from the things that dishonor you. In Jesus' name we pray. Amen.

Share Reflections | 5 min.

Have each person share one reflection from the Reflect exercise on the first page of the Individual Study. You can do this in pairs, or in the larger group if you have time. This is not a time to critique or ask lots of questions of each other, but simply to share something God has put on your heart.

Clarify Issues from the Lesson | 10 min.

Back in the larger group, prepare for your discussion by clarifying any uncertainties about the Scripture or commentary, but be careful with your time. The purpose here is to focus on a few issues that may be par-ticularly difficult, not to open a broad discussion about the lesson.

Meaning of Leviticus for Today | 20 min.

Take turns reading aloud each point below, and discuss the questions as a group:

A. Holiness in the Midst of Our Culture—The ritual states of Old Testament Israel and the laws for careful treatment of the Lord's most holy offerings in Lev. 6:24-7:10 taught Israel the importance of distinguishing between the holy and profane in all aspects of their lives. The New Testament carries forward this same concern for the Church's holiness or being "set apart" from the world (Jn. 17:6-19; 1 Cor. 7:29-31; 2 Cor. 6:14-7:1; Phil. 2:14-16; 2 Tim. 2:20-22; Jm. 1:27; 1 Pet. 1:13-16; 1 Jn. 2:15-17).

1. Discuss some of the more significant ways the Church, and we as individual believers, fail to honor the Lord's command to be "set apart" from the world:

2. While the New Testament emphasizes our being "set apart," it also emphasizes that God is *not* calling us to remove ourselves from or even to judge the non-believing world (1 Cor. 5:6-13). Jesus has called us to remain in the world to testify to his Lordship and to make disciples of all the nations (Mt. 28:18-20). Discuss several ways the Church tends to get this backwards—that is, ways in which we tend to separate ourselves from and judge the non-believing world, rather than testifying to Jesus and making disciples:

B. Providing for the Church's Leaders—Israel's laws for distributing the "most holy" portions of the purification and reparation offerings (Lev. 7:7) and various portions of the burnt and grain offerings (7:8-10) helped meet the practical needs of the priests who served as the community's worship leaders and intercessors. The New Testament carries forward this same command to the Church to meet the practical needs of its shepherds. See 1 Cor. 9:13-14; Gal. 6:6; 1 Tim. 5:7. **Discuss ways the local church can help meet the financial needs of its pastor(s) so they can continue caring for the Lord's people:**

EVALUATE

Witnessing in Holiness | 20 min.

In 1 Cor. 5:6-13, Paul is clear that we not called to disassociate ourselves from the unbelieving world, but rather to "purge the evil from among" us. In other words, the Church's calling to reflect God's holiness in the unbelieving culture *is the way* we are to be "set apart" from the world. Being set apart requires the Church to pursue *corporate holiness*, so our witness in the culture is pure and honoring to the Lord. **Brainstorm some practical steps your church could take to actively pursue corporate holiness in your local community.**

PROPER WORSHIP: PURIFICATION AND FELLOWSHIP OFFERINGS

ENGAGE

Reflect

Write a few notes about how you tend to spend your time with the Lord. Is it primarily focused on prayer for others or for yourself and your needs? How much time and focus do you devote to acknowledging the Lord's character and his great redemption of his people? How much time and focus do you devote to praising and thanking him for his love and goodness toward you and those you love?

Pray

Heavenly Father, as I study your word in Leviticus, I pray that you would shape my heart and will so I would seek to praise you in all things and to publicly give you thanks in the midst of your people. In Jesus' name I pray. Amen.

Read

- Read Lev. 7:11-38, which concerns proper handling of the fellowship offering (traditionally, "peace offering"), as well as three types of fellowship offerings: the praise, vow, and freewill offerings. It also provides a summary (7:37-36) that closes out the first two sections of Leviticus (1:1-6:7, and 6:8-7:36), both of which deal with the five major offerings.
- In the commentary, review "Context" (126-127). For the name "fellowship offering" (instead of "peace offering"), review comment on 3:11 (pp. 104-105, especially p. 105 footnote 6).
- Read Lev. 7:11-38 again.

A. Laws for the Fellowship Offerings—Read "Comment" on Lev. 7:11-18 (133-136): Leviticus 3 introduced the fellowship offering (translated "peace offering" in many Bibles; see at 3:11). This section of Leviticus 7 introduces three different types of fellowship offerings: the *praise* offering (7:12-15) and *vow* and *freewill* offerings (7:16-18).

1. Briefly describe the *purposes* of the praise, vow, and freewill fellowship offerings:

2. The *praise* fellowship offering required a more elaborate set of breads than the other fellowship offerings, and sacrificial meat from a praise offering had to be eaten the day it was offered, perhaps to guard it from becoming ritually defiled through improper handling. What do these two requirements suggest about the praise fellowship offering?

3. When Israelites made vows, they promised the Lord they would carry out certain tasks if and when he answered their prayers. This was not, however, a way of buying the Lord's help. What two functions, then, did vows or promises serve?

4. What purpose was served by the fact that the vow fellowship offering was made publicly?

5. The *freewill* fellowship offering was not made to fulfill a promise, as with the vow offering, or because the Lord had answered a specific prayer, as with the praise offering. What, then, might an Israelite have been expressing by bringing a freewill fellowship offering?

B. Ritual Purity and the Fellowship Offering—Read "Comment" on Lev. 7:19-21 (136). The law of the fellowship offering regulated when sacrificial meat could and could not be eaten (7:15-18). This section concerns two additional cases when meat from the fellowship offering was <u>not</u> to be eaten.

1. The first case involved sacrificial meat *touching something ritually impure*. Why would this mean that the meat couldn't be eaten?

2. The second case involved the *worshippers themselves being ritually impure*, either through various activities or health conditions or from contact with something ritually impure. Why was it unlawful for a ritually impure worshipper to eat meat from a sacrificial offering?

3. The penalty for eating the meat of a fellowship offering in a ritually impure state was to be *cut off* from the people of Israel (Lev. 7:20-21)—a very serious penalty. What two ways might an Israelite be cut off from the people?

C. Priests' Portions of the Fellowship Offerings—Read "Comment" on Lev. 7:22-27 and 7:28-36 (137-138). This section of Leviticus 7 regulates how various portions of the fellowship offerings were to be given to the Lord and distributed among the priests.

1. Since Israelite worshippers were permitted to eat portions of the fellowship offerings, they only needed to bring *parts* of the offerings to the Lord. These included the fat as the very best portion to honor the Lord and the blood to acknowledge his sovereignty over all of life. What were the *other two portions* and the names of the offerings made from them (Lev. 7:30, 32)?

2. Identify two reasons why the Israelites would have considered the right thigh of the fellowship "contribution offering" to have been particularly valuable?

A. Honoring Our Spiritual Leaders—Read "Meaning" (138-139). The Lord required that some of the best portions of the fellowship offerings—the breast of the wave offering and right thigh of the contribution offering—were to be given to the priests and their families as their "perpetual share from the people of Israel… throughout their generations" (Lev. 7:34, 36). This was almost certainly intended to teach the Israelites that they were to honor their spiritual leaders.

1. One of the ways in which we are to honor our spiritual leaders today is to make sure they are cared for financially (Gal. 6:6; 1 Tim. 5:17). But the New Testament also exhorts us to honor them by submitting to their authority (Heb. 13:17; 1 Pet. 5:5). Describe one or two examples of ways we can submit to our spiritual leaders—pastors, elders, lay ministers—that honors them:

2. The New Testament is also clear that submission to spiritual leaders should be done in a way that contributes to their joy. While they are called to shepherd us willingly and eagerly (1 Pet. 5:2), we are called to be the kind of "sheep" that are a joy to shepherd (Heb. 13:17b). Describe one or two ways we might formally submit to our spiritual leaders but would <u>not</u> contribute to their joy?

B. Offering Praise in Our Fellowship—The praise offering (Lev. 7:12-15) was perhaps the most sacred of the fellowship offerings (see "Comment", 134-135). The Hebrew word used in those verses for "praise" or "thankfulness" is *todah*, which refers to worshipfully acknowledging the Lord for his deeds. **Describe one or two concrete ways we might make our own "praise offerings" to the Lord as we gather in various forms of fellowship (shared meals, ministry meetings, small group studies, social activities, etc.):**

RESPOND

Meditate—Meditate on Psalm 111 each day this week as you reflect on the sacredness of the praise fellowship offering and its purpose in worshipfully acknowledging the Lord for his deeds. Spend time reflecting on his great deeds on your behalf and on behalf of your believing family and/or friends, as members of his covenant family.

Take Action—The Israelites gave praise fellowship offerings to the Lord in response to specific prayers he had answered (see "Comment", 134). As you meditate on Psalm 111 this week, make a list of specific prayers you are offering up to the Lord. Keep the list in a prominent place to help keep your prayers in mind. When the Lord answers a prayer—with a "yes" or "no" or perhaps a "wait"—be sure to offer him praise for his answer. When possible, offer your praise in the context of fellowship with others.

PROPER WORSHIP: PURIFICATION AND FELLOWSHIP OFFERINGS

ANALYZE

Opening Prayer

Heavenly Father, as we study your word in Leviticus, we pray that you would shape our hearts and wills so we would seek to praise you in all things and to publicly give you thanks in the midst of your people. In Jesus' name we pray. Amen.

Share Reflections | 5 min.

Have each person share one reflection from the Reflect exercise on the first page of the Individual Study. You can do this in pairs, or in the larger group if you have time. This is not a time to critique or ask lots of questions of each other, but simply to share something God has put on your heart.

Clarify Issues from the Lesson | 10 min.

Back in the larger group, prepare for your discussion by clarifying any uncertainties about the Scripture or commentary, but be careful with your time. The purpose here is to focus on a few issues that may be particularly difficult, not to open a broad discussion about the lesson.

Meaning of Leviticus for Today | 20 min.

Take turns reading aloud each point below, and discuss the questions as a group:

A. Ritual Purity and New Testament Communion—In Israel, a worshipper could become ritually impure through various activities or health conditions or from contact with something ritually impure. Israelites in a state of ritual impurity were forbidden from participating in the fellowship offering (7:19-21). This prohibition was so serious that violating it carried the penalty of being cut off from the people of God. The New Testament carries forward the concern for purity in connection with the Lord's Supper, the fellowship meal of the New Covenant community. For example, Paul says we are not to partake in communion in "an unworthy manner" (1 Cor. 11:27). In this context, however, the focus is not on ritual impurity, but on moral impurity. Specifically, Paul is referring to our partaking of communion when we have treated others in the covenant community with disdain and have not repented (1 Cor. 11:20-22). This is tantamount to mocking the very thing the communion meal represents: the body and blood of Christ by which we and our covenant brothers and sisters enter into relationship with him (1 Cor. 10:16-17; 11:27).

1. Discuss two or three implications of this New Testament warning for individual worshippers as they partake of communion:

2. Discuss two or three implications of this New Testament warning for the manner in which communion should be officiated and conducted:

B. Honoring Our Spiritual Leaders—The Lord required that some of the best portions of the fellowship offerings—the breast of the wave offering and right thigh of the contribution offering—were to be given to the priests and their families as their "perpetual share from the people of Israel" (Lev. 7:34). This was almost certainly intended to teach the Israelites that they were to honor their spiritual leaders. The New Testament likewise exhorts us to honor our spiritual leaders in various ways, including by submitting to their authority (Heb. 13:17; 1 Pet. 5:5).

1. Discuss specific ways in which members of your community can serve with their own unique spiritual gifts and still honor your spiritual leaders by submitting to their authority:

2. Discuss specific ways, other than those implied by the previous discussion, in which a church's members can dishonor their spiritual leaders by failing or refusing to submit to their authority:

Helping Our Leaders Shepherd with Joy | 20 min.

The New Testament is clear that submission to spiritual leaders should be done in a way that contributes to their joy. While they are called to shepherd us willingly and eagerly (1 Pet. 5:2), we are called to be the kind of "sheep" that are a joy to shepherd (Heb. 13:17b). **Brainstorm some practical steps that members of your community could take that would increase the joy with which your spiritual leaders are shepherding the community. Make a plan for pursuing your ideas and follow through with it:**

LEVITICUS 8

ORDINATION OF THE PRIESTS FOR PUBLIC WORSHIP

ENGAGE

Reflect

Imagine trying to secure an invitation to a White House dinner with the President of the United States. How would you go about pursuing such an invitation? Do you know the President personally? If not, do you have any contacts powerful enough to secure an invitation for you? If you can't even secure an invitation to dinner with the President, how can you hope to get an invitation to the banquet table of the God of the universe (Rev. 19:9)?

Pray

Heavenly Father, as I study your word in Leviticus, I pray you would grow my devotion to your son, Jesus, the mediator to me of your great salvation, and help me to rest in the assurance that he has opened my way into your holy presence through the blood of his sacrifice on the cross. In Jesus' name I pray. Amen.

Read

- Read Leviticus 8, which introduces the beginning of Israel's worship of the Lord at the tabernacle. Specifically, Leviticus 8 concerns the ordination of the high priest Aaron and his sons, who were to officiate public worship before the Lord as Israel's priests.
- In the commentary, read "Context" (141-142), and "Introduction," section 5.d (69-71).
- Read Leviticus 8 again.

A. Ordination of Aaron, the High Priest—Review "Context" (141-142) and read "Comment" on Lev. 8:1-13 (142-145): This section of Leviticus 8 concerns preparations the Lord commanded Moses to make for the ordination of the priests and the initial ordination rites for the high priest, Aaron, and his sons.

1. Ceremonies bring about a change in status for the main participants through a series of rites or rituals related to its purpose. The ordination of spiritual leaders is a type of ceremony. Briefly describe the purpose of the ordination ceremony for Aaron and his sons:

2. Why was the ordination ceremony to take place at the tent of meeting entrance (8:3-4)?

3. Briefly describe the significance of the washing of Aaron and his sons with water (8:6)?

4. Briefly describe the significance of the special clothing Moses dressed Aaron in (8:7-9)?

5. The high priest's clothing was more elaborate than that of the other priests, setting him apart as their leader. It also had royal overtones (robes, blue cloth, turban, crown). What would such royal clothing have signified to the Israelites?

6. After washing and dressing Aaron, Moses then anointed and thus consecrated (made holy) the tent of meeting and everything in it. Why was this necessary?

7. After anointing the tent of meeting, Moses finally anointed all the objects in the courtyard surrounding the tent. What was the significance that the entire tabernacle complex had now been consecrated?

B. Special Offerings for Ordination and Consecration—Read "Comment" on Lev. 8:14-36 (146-148). This section concerns special offerings and instructions required for the ordination and final consecration of Aaron and his sons. The offerings were the purification, burnt, and ordination offerings:

1. Moses presented the purification offering before presenting the other offerings. Why would this have been a logical order?

2. Aaron and his sons laid their hands on the head of the purification offering, indicating it was being made on their behalf. What did this signify in terms of the priests' relationship to other Israelites?

3. Why is it appropriate that the ordination offering was a type of fellowship offering?

C. God's Initiation of Relationship—Read "Meaning" (148-149). The Lord is the one who initiates the relationship between Israel and himself. Here in Leviticus 8, he is the one who commands Moses to provide a means for Israel to come into his holy presence and worship him (8:1-15). But this also presented an immediate problem because the Lord's holiness destroys impurity and sinfulness, making it potentially lethal to be in his presence. Thus, in Leviticus 8, he provides a way to safely come before him.

1. What did the Lord communicate by commanding that the priests' ordination take place before all the Israelites?

2. What did the Lord communicate by providing the priests as mediators?

APPLY

A. The Perfect High Priest—The ordination ceremony of Leviticus 8 established Aaron and his sons as priestly mediators between Israel and the Lord. But the fact that the Lord commanded Moses to offer sacrifices for Aaron and his sons made it clear that the priests were just as sinful as the rest of Israel, and needed atonement for their own sins. Thankfully, we now have a perfect high priest in Jesus.

1. What does Heb. 7:26-27 say about Jesus' nature and service as high priest that distinguishes him from Aaron and all the other high priests?

2. Moses consecrated Aaron as high priest and mediator for the people by, among other things, sprinkling blood from the sacrifices on him (8:30) because the blood of sacrificial offerings is the powerful ritual agent chosen by God for purification from sin. See "Comment" (146). What does Heb. 9:11-15 say about the blood by which Jesus—the final mediator for sin—"entered once for all into the holy places" (Heb. 9:12)?

3. To enter into the holy presence of the Lord, Aaron was washed with ritually purifying water (8:6; "Comment", 142) and sprinkled with ritually purifying blood (8:30; "Comment", 147-148). What does Heb. 10:19-22 say about our access into the Lord's holy presence because of the "sprinkling" and "washing" we have received through Christ?

RESPOND

Meditate—Meditate on Heb. 10:19-25 this week. Reflect especially on the riches God has provided us in Christ, our mediator of his salvation toward us: Confidence to enter God's holy presence (v. 19), a great high priest over God's church, and (v. 21) hearts cleansed by Christ's blood with which we can come before God in full assurance that we are accepted by faith in Christ (v. 22).

Take Action—The meditation passage for this week, Heb. 10:19-25, entails great truths about our acceptance before the Lord through Jesus. But it also entails commands concerning how we are to respond to these truths. Verses 24-25 command us to not neglect meeting together so we can encourage one another "to love and good works." Spend time reflecting on your obedience to this command, write out a few concrete, practical steps for ordering your life in a way that allows you to walk in greater obedience to it, and begin taking some of those steps this week.

ORDINATION OF THE PRIESTS
FOR PUBLIC WORSHIP

ANALYZE

Opening Prayer

Heavenly Father, as we study your word in Leviticus, we pray you would grow devotion in our hearts for your son, Jesus, the mediator of your great salvation to us, and help us to rest in the assurance that he has opened the way into your holy presence through the blood of his sacrifice on the cross. In Jesus' name we pray. Amen.

Share Reflections | 5 min.

Have each person share one reflection from the Reflect exercise on the first page of the Individual Study. You can do this in pairs, or in the larger group if you have time. This is not a time to critique or ask lots of questions of each other, but simply to share something God has put on your heart.

Clarify Issues from the Lesson | 10 min.

Back in the larger group, prepare for your discussion by clarifying any uncertainties about the Scripture or commentary, but be careful with your time. The purpose here is to focus on a few issues that may be particularly difficult, not to open a broad discussion about the lesson.

Meaning of Leviticus for Today | 20 min.

Take turns reading aloud each point below, and discuss the questions as a group:

A. Meeting Together in the Lord's Presence Through Jesus—The book of Hebrews is perhaps the single clearest Scripture describing the rich and complex ways Jesus has become our "great high priest" (Heb. 10:21), who has "entered once and for all into the holy places, not by means of the blood of goats and calves, but by means of his own blood, thus securing an eternal redemption" for those of us who believe (Heb. 9:12). Hebrews 10:19-22 sets forth the awesome truth that we can come confidently into the Lord's holy presence because of Jesus' mediating work on our behalf. But the following verses also set forth the expected response to this great truth: We are to hold fast to the testimony of our hope, not neglect meeting together, and thereby encourage one another to "love and good works" (Heb. 10:23-25).

1. Discuss ways your church community might excel even more in terms of encouraging one another to hold fast to their hope and to love and good works by "not neglecting" to meet together:

B. God's Holy Temple—The fact that the Lord set apart a holy place to dwell in the midst of his people was a reminder of the same desire he showed in the Garden of Eden: to dwell with his people and walk among them. In the New Testament, the Lord shows this same desire in and through his Son Jesus, through whom he has now and forever consecrated his people to be his holy temple in which his Spirit dwells (1 Cor. 3:16).

1. In 2 Cor. 6:14-18, Paul reminds us we are the "living temple of God," and admonishes us to "not be unequally yoked with unbelievers" but to "go out from their midst and be separate from them" (quoting Isa. 52:11). Yet in his same letter to the Corinthian church, Paul is also clear that God has given us the "ministry of reconciliation" to the world as "ambassadors for Christ" (2 Cor. 5:18-20). Discuss ways we —as individual followers of Christ and corporately as the Church—can faithfully pursue this ministry of reconciliation to the world while we remain separate or "consecrated" from the world.

Testimonies of a Holy Priesthood | 20 min.

The ordination ceremony of Leviticus 8 established Aaron and his descendants as the members of the priesthood. But now in the New Covenant, the Lord has established all those united with Christ as a "royal priesthood, a holy nation, a people for his own possession, that [we] may proclaim the excellencies of him who has called [us] out of darkness into his marvelous light" (1 Pet. 2:9). **Brainstorm ways your church and its ministries might function as the Lord's "royal priesthood" by proclaiming God's excellence and worthiness through our testimonies of being called from darkness to light.** List several concrete steps your church or small group could take, and make a plan for helping it follow through with those steps:

LEVITICUS 9

THE BEGINNING OF PUBLIC WORSHIP AND THE LORD'S APPEARANCE IN GLORY

ENGAGE

Reflect

Write down several ways in which you "know" those to whom you are closest. How have you gotten to "know" them? What aspects of your relationships have contributed to your knowing them better over time? What aspects have perhaps detracted from this? Now write several reflections on these same aspects of your relationship with Christ and your "knowing" him:

Pray

Heavenly Father, as I study your word in Leviticus, I pray you would deepen in me an ongoing sense of awe and respect for your glory and draw me closer to your Son Jesus that I might know him more intimately with each passing day. In Jesus' name I pray. Amen.

Read

- Read Leviticus 9, which concerns the inauguration of Israel's public worship and the Lord's first appearance to all Israel, signaling his acceptance of their worship and desire to dwell in covenant relationship with them.
- In the commentary, read "Context" (149-150).
- Read Leviticus 9 again.

A. Preparing for the Inauguration Ceremony—Review "Context" (149-150), and read "Comment" on Lev. 9:1-5 (150). While Leviticus chapters 1-7 concern the offerings presented in public worship and chapter 8 concerns ordination of the priests who present those offerings on the people's behalf, chapter 9 concerns the inauguration of public worship itself.

1. The inauguration of Israel's worship was a highly significant event, marked by a special preparation ceremony. For what in particular were the priests and people preparing themselves?

2. Leviticus 9 reaches its peak with the Lord, Israel's covenant King, appearing in all his glory and accepting the people's sacrifices. What two things in particular did this signify to them?

3. Lev. 9:1-5 specifies the preparations the Lord commanded Moses to make for the inauguration ceremony. Among them were two sets of offerings. On whose behalf were each of these made?

4. The sacrifices followed the order of purification offering, burnt offering, and finally, fellowship offering. Briefly describe the purpose of each as presented in this order:

5. As Moses and the priests brought the offerings to the tent of meeting, all Israel came near and stood before the Lord, which is language used to describe one person standing before a ruler or someone in authority. What were the two purposes for standing before the Lord in this ceremony?

B. The Inauguration Ceremony Commences—Read "Comment" on Lev. 9:6-22 (151-154). This section concerns the presentation of the inauguration offerings the Lord had specified to Moses.

1. With all Israel gathered, Moses explained what the Lord had commanded be done so that his glory might appear to Israel—that is, so the Lord might *demonstrate his presence* to Israel in a spectacular way. Why is such a display of his presence described as *the glory of the Lord*?

2. The sacrifices offered at the inauguration were an impressive range of costly animals, which deviated from the typical sacrifices of Lev. 1-7. For example, Aaron was to offer a *calf*, rather than an adult bull, for the purification offering and a calf and a *lamb* for the burnt offering. Young animals, such as calves and lambs, were considered culinary delicacies and thus more valuable than adult animals. Why did the Lord command these special animals for this occasion?

3. When the offerings had been made, Aaron *lifted his hands* towards the people and blessed them, which was the specific duty of the priest. Describe the *nature* of the blessing and who carried it out:

C. The Lord's Appearance at the Inauguration—Read "Comment" on Lev. 9:23-24 (154). The inauguration ceremony of Leviticus 9 culminated in the appearance of the Lord's glory.

1. In Lev. 9:23, we learn Moses and Aaron entered the tent of meeting after Aaron had presented all the offerings and blessed the people. What two inferences might we draw from both of them entering the tent of meeting?

2. Leviticus 9:23 also tells us the glory of the Lord appeared to the people after Moses and Aaron came out of the tent of meeting and blessed them. How did the Lord's glory manifest itself, according to Lev. 9:24, and how else might it have manifested itself in this situation?

3. Describe the two ways the people responded to the appearance of the Lord's glory:

APPLY

A. The Lord's Acceptance of Israel's Offerings—Read "Meaning" (154-155). The Lord's spectacular display of his presence—the revealing of his glory—demonstrated to the Israelites that he was dwelling in their midst and receiving their worship.

1. The first implication of the Lord's glory appearing to Israel is that *the priesthood was working* ("Meaning," 154-155). Aaron had been allowed to enter the tent of meeting (Lev. 9:23), thus signaling that the Lord had accepted Israel's new high priest as their mediator to offer atoning sacrifices for their sin ("Comment," 154). How do Heb. 9:24 and 10:12 depict the Lord's acceptance of Jesus as the final high priest and mediator of our atonement, once for all?

2. The second implication of the Lord's glory appearing to Israel is that *he desired the Israelites to know him* as their covenant King and experience the blessing of relationship with him. Jesus came to dwell with us in order to reveal the Lord's ultimate glory (Jn. 1:14) and to open the way for relationship with God (Jn. 1:12; Heb. 10:19-22) ("Meaning," 155). How does Jesus' high priestly prayer in Jn. 17:3 and 17:20-21 express this same desire of the Lord that we *know him* and *experience relationship* with him?

B. The Purpose of the Appearance of the Lord's Glory—Review "Meaning" (155). The Lord's spectacular display of his presence demonstrated to Israel his awesome power and might. Those who witnessed it could not help but give him glory and honor, shouting out with joy at his goodness and greatness (9:24). The Lord displayed his power and might not just to elicit worship from the Israelites but to instill in their hearts a proper reverence for – and even fear – of him. Leviticus 9:24 tells us that when the Lord's glory appeared, "fire came out from before the Lord and consumed" the offerings on the altar. Hebrews 12:28-29 refers to the Lord as "a consuming fire". **What two responses does the book of Hebrews command?**

RESPOND

Meditate—Meditate this week on Jesus' high priestly prayer in John 17, especially as he prays that his disciples might know him and his Father and be united with them in relationship. Remember as you reflect on his prayer that Jesus prayed it for you personally, not just for his first disciples (Jn. 17:20-21).

Take Action—In Phil. 3:7-11, Paul shares with the Philippians his desire to know Christ, which is one of the fundamental reasons the Lord appeared and manifested his glory ("Meaning," 155; Jn. 17:3; 1 Jn. 1:1-3). Paul considers several aspects of "knowing Christ" that entail "counting" everything Paul once relied on as "loss" (v. 8), receiving Christ's righteousness through faith (v. 9), and sharing in his sufferings (v. 10). Spend some time reflecting on the things you rely on in life, your acceptance of Christ's righteousness on your behalf, and your willingness to enter into his sufferings. Which of these are furthering your knowing Christ in the way Paul describes? Which may be hindering your knowing him in this way? Write down a few concrete, practical steps you might take to "forget what lies behind" and "press on toward the goal" of knowing Christ all the more (Phil. 3:13-14). Take some of those steps this week.

THE BEGINNING OF PUBLIC WORSHIP AND THE LORD'S APPEARANCE IN GLORY

ANALYZE

Opening Prayer

Heavenly Father, as we study your word in Leviticus, we pray you would deepen in us an ongoing sense of awe and respect for your glory and draw us closer to your Son Jesus that we might know him more intimately with each passing day. In Jesus' name we pray. Amen.

Share Reflections | 5 min.

Have each person share one reflection from the Reflect exercise on the first page of the Individual Study. You can do this in pairs, or in the larger group if you have time. This is not a time to critique or ask lots of questions of each other, but simply to share something God has put on your heart.

Clarify Issues from the Lesson | 10 min.

Back in the larger group, prepare for your discussion by clarifying any uncertainties about the Scripture or commentary, but be careful with your time. The purpose here is to focus on a few issues that may be particularly difficult, not to open a broad discussion about the lesson.

Meaning of Leviticus for Today | 20 min.

Take turns reading aloud each point below, and discuss the questions as a group:

A. Proper Response to the Glory of the Lord—The Lord's spectacular display of his presence demonstrated to Israel his awesome power and might—that is, his glory—and caused the assembly to shout for joy and fall face down to the ground (Lev. 9:24). These responses reflect two purposes for the Lord's manifesting his presence to us: that we (a) give him glory and honor *with joy* for his goodness and greatness, and (b) cultivate in our hearts a *proper reverence* (Prov. 1:7, "fear") for him. **Discuss some ways your church's corporate worship or small group gathering might be structured or conducted to equip, facilitate, and encourage its members in these two responses of joyful and reverent honoring of the Lord:**

B. Blessing the People—Twice during the inauguration ceremony of Leviticus 9 we are told Moses and Aaron blessed the people. After offering all the sacrifices Moses had commanded, Aaron lifted his hands and blessed the people (9:22). Moses and Aaron then went into the tent of meeting, and when they came out, they blessed the people and *then the glory of the Lord appeared* (9:23). The blessings were actually prayers for the people, and the Lord was the one who did the blessing ("Comment," 153). Peter says we are a "royal priesthood" (1 Pet. 2:9) called to bless others even when they treat us poorly (1 Pet 3:9). **Discuss some examples of how and when it may be challenging to bless one another this way in the local church and some responses to each challenge that are in line with Peter's admonition:**

CREATE

The Appearing of the Lord and His Glory | 20 min.

One of the implications of the Lord's glory appearing to Israel is that *he desired the Israelites to know him* as their covenant King and experience the blessing of relationship with him. Jesus' high priestly prayer in Jn. 17:3 and 17:20-21 expresses this same desire of the Lord that we *know him and experience relationship* with him. **Brainstorm some concrete ways in which your church and its ministries, as the body of Christ (1 Cor. 12:27; Eph. 4:12), might excel even more in being a living manifestation of the "appearing" of the Lord (2 Cor. 4:10-11).** Remember the purpose of doing this is so those in your church community and the non-believing community at large might know Jesus. Make a plan for sharing your ideas with others in your church:

THE LORD'S JUDGMENT ON UNFAITHFUL PRIESTS, HIS WARNING TO AARON, AND AARON'S FAITHFULNESS

ENGAGE

Reflect

Make a short list of your "character flaws" or "opportunities for growth" that others have brought to your attention over the years. Now go through the list and write a few reflections about how these critiques make you feel and the extent to which you've acknowledged them as valid and have taken steps to address them:

Pray

Heavenly Father, as I study your word in Leviticus, I pray you would make me sensitive to your discipline in my life, so I might seek your forgiveness and genuinely repent of the sin that impedes my fellowship with you and your Son Jesus, my faithful high priest, in whose name I pray. Amen.

Read

- Read Leviticus 10, which concerns the Lord's judgment against Aaron's sons for unfaithfulness in their priestly duties, his further warnings to Aaron and his other sons, and Aaron's faithfulness in the midst of these events.
- In the commentary, read "Context" (155-156), and review diagram of the tabernacle, 86.
- Read Leviticus 10 again.

UNDERSTAND

A. The Lord Judges Aaron's Sons for Grave Disrespect—Read "Comment" on Lev. 10:1-7 (156-159). This section of Leviticus 10 concerns the Lord's judgment against two of Aaron's sons, Nadab and Abihu, for grave breach of their priestly duties and disrespecting the Lord himself.

1. Leviticus 10:1 says Nadab and Abihu offered "unauthorized fire" before the Lord. Leviticus 16 provides additional context for understanding this event. What are the two likely aspects of their sin before the Lord?

2. By attempting to make an offering at a time of their own choosing and apparently in the Lord's very throne room without explicit invitation, Nadab and Abihu committed a severe breach of royal protocol (cf. Esth. 4:11). What else did their misconduct signify?

3. The events of Leviticus 9, the priests' inauguration, and the episode with Nadab and Abihu moved Israel from triumph to tragedy in a single day. How was "fire" a key element in this dramatic reversal?

4. After the deaths of Nadab and Abihu, the Lord spoke to Aaron through Moses and explained he would "show himself holy" among those who approach him (that is, the priests) and "display his glory" publicly in sight of all his people (Lev. 10:3). These same words are used elsewhere in the context of miracles from God with two purposes in mind. Briefly describe in your own words these two purposes:

5. Aaron and his remaining sons were prohibited from observing the expected mourning rites for Nadab and Abihu (Lev. 10:6-7) because they had been set apart into a special status of holiness during the ordination and inauguration ceremonies. Why did this special status prohibit them from mourning?

B. The Lord Warns Aaron Directly—Read "Comment" on Lev. 10:8-11 (159-160). The Lord speaks directly to Aaron alone this one time in Leviticus, warning him that the priests must not drink wine or other alcoholic beverages when performing their duties in the sanctuary. He gives three reasons:

1. The first reason was so Aaron and his sons *would not die*. Briefly explain how drinking alcohol while "on duty" might lead to their deaths:

2. The second reason was so Aaron and his sons could *properly distinguish between ritual categories*. Briefly explain why this was so vitally important:

3. The third reason was so Aaron and his sons could *clearly teach the Israelites the decrees of the Lord*. Briefly describe two ways alcohol consumption could hamper the priests from properly teaching the people the ways of the Lord:

C. Aaron's Faithfulness Before the Lord—Read "Comment" on Lev. 10:12-20 (160-161). This section of Leviticus 10 concerns Moses' fear that Aaron's remaining sons, Eleazar and Ithamar, had just repeated the tragic sin of their late brothers by improperly handling the purification offering.

1. Moses was concerned because Aaron's sons had not eaten the meat of the purification offering. This would mean the offering had not been performed properly and that the Lord would not accept it. Why was the Lord's acceptance so important?

2. But Moses and Aaron had made two different assumptions about this particular purification offering. Briefly describe their two different assumptions and how those assumptions affected whether Aaron's sons had sinned in the matter:

APPLY

A. The Awesome Responsibility of the Priesthood—Read "Meaning" (162). A major theme of Leviticus 10 is the awesome responsibility of Israel's priests as the spiritual leaders of God's people. This responsibility is seen in at least two respects: First, the priests were to follow the Lord's commands exactly and so honor him as their King. Second, the priests were responsible for leading the Israelites spiritually, guiding them in their covenant relationship with their covenant King by following his covenant laws. The New Testament reflects this concern by affirming that those who teach God's people are held to a higher account than others (Jas. 3:1) because they are responsible for the spiritual safety of those they lead (162).

1. Identify one or two situations in a church or small group setting in which failing to hold leaders accountable might lead to spiritual, emotional, or even physical harm to those they lead:

2. How does Jesus describe himself in Jn. 5:19 as following the Lord's commands as our "great high priest" (Heb. 4:14)?

B. The Lord's Judgment as Mercy On His People—Review "Comment" (159). The Lord's judgment against Nadab and Abihu and his further warnings to Aaron were not the capricious responses of a quick-tempered deity. Rather, they were meant to underscore to the Israelites his holy hatred of sin and to alert them to the presence of evil in their midst so they could address it properly and maintain their life-giving fellowship with him. **How does the apostle Paul apply this same principle in his discipline of the Corinthian church in 1 Cor. 5:1-13 (see esp. vv. 1-5)?**

Meditate—The Lord's discipline is a form of his merciful judgment (1 Cor. 11:32) that alerts us to sin in our lives that we need to address in order to maintain our rich fellowship with him. Meditate this week on Heb. 12:1-11, where we are called to lay aside the sin that so easily entangles us and to look to Jesus, the founder and perfecter of our faith, even while the Lord "disciplines us for our good, that we may share in his holiness" (Heb. 12:10).

Take Action—When the Lord draws attention to sin in the midst of his people, he expects us to take steps to properly address it, including asking his forgiveness and pursuing genuine repentance (1 Jn. 1:9; 2 Cor. 7:9-10). As you meditate this week on Heb. 12:1-11, take time to reflect on whether the Lord may be bringing discipline into your life at any points for sins of which you may not have fully repented. If the Holy Spirit brings any such sins to your mind, write down a few concrete, practical steps you can take to move toward complete repentance and begin taking those steps this week.

LEVITICUS 10

THE LORD'S JUDGMENT ON UNFAITHFUL PRIESTS, HIS WARNING TO AARON, AND AARON'S FAITHFULNESS

ANALYZE

Opening Prayer

Heavenly Father, as we study your word in Leviticus, we pray you would make us sensitive to your discipline in our lives, so we might seek your forgiveness and genuinely repent of the sin that impedes our fellowship with you and your Son Jesus, our faithful high priest, in whose name we pray. Amen.

Share Reflections | 5 min.

Have each person share one reflection from the Reflect exercise on the first page of the Individual Study. You can do this in pairs, or in the larger group if you have time. This is not a time to critique or ask lots of questions of each other, but simply to share something God has put on your heart.

Clarify Issues from the Lesson | 10 min.

Back in the larger group, prepare for your discussion by clarifying any uncertainties about the Scripture or commentary, but be careful with your time. The purpose here is to focus on a few issues that may be particularly difficult, not to open a broad discussion about the lesson.

Meaning of Leviticus for Today | 20 min.

Take turns reading aloud each point below, and discuss the questions as a group:

A. The Lord's Judgment as Mercy on His People—The Lord's judgment against Nadab and Abihu and his further warnings to Aaron in Leviticus 10 were meant to underscore the Lord's holy hatred of sin and to alert Israel to the presence of evil in her midst so the people could address it properly and maintain their life-giving fellowship with him. Paul applies this same principle in 1 Cor. 5:1-13 concerning sexual immorality in the midst of the Corinthian church and the need to "cleanse out the old leaven" (v. 7) and "purge the evil person from among you" (v. 13). The Holy Spirit judged Ananias and Sapphira with death in Acts 5:1-11 for withholding their possessions from the congregation while lying about it. "And great fear came upon the whole church and upon all who heard of these things" (v. 11). **Discuss some contemporary examples in the American church where God may choose to judge**

individual members, or perhaps entire congregations, for serious sin in their midst that could lead others astray in their fellowship with the Lord or away from coming to belief in him:

B. Avoiding Impairment in Spiritual Leaders' Judgment—In Lev. 10:8-11, the Lord warned Aaron directly against the priests drinking wine or other alcoholic beverages when performing their duties in the sanctuary. He gave several reasons, including the need for the priests to distinguish between the holy and common and to properly teach the Lord's decrees to the people. The command's aim, then, was to ensure that the spiritual leaders' judgment, discernment, and modeling to the community was not impaired in any way. The misuse of alcohol or other controlled substances is an obvious danger in this regard, and the explicit subject of the Lord's commands in Leviticus 10. But spiritual leaders' judgment, discernment, and modeling to the community may be impaired by other means. **Discuss some concrete examples of these and also ways in which leaders and other members of the community might help guard against these dangers.**

CREATE

Asking For Mercy and Grace in Our Time of Need | 20 min.

The author of Hebrews encourages us that "we do not have a high priest who is unable to sympathize with our weaknesses, but one who in every respect has been tempted as we are, yet without sin" (Heb. 4:15). Therefore, we are to "with confidence draw near to the throne of grace, that we may receive mercy and find grace to help in time of need" (Heb. 4:16). In light of the previous discussion question, spend time now in your small group praying for your church's spiritual leaders—pastors, elders, directors, staff, teachers and others. Intercede for them by asking for mercy and grace that they might be saved from specific dangers and temptations that would impair their judgment and for discernment that they may continue serving as examples to the community in their vital function of leading others to "be holy as the Lord is holy" (1 Pet. 1:15-16) and teaching others in the ways of the Lord (1 Tim. 4:16; Tit. 2:7-8).

Laws on Pure and Impure Creatures, and How Israel is to Relate to Them

ENGAGE

Reflect

Take a few minutes to reflect on how your life looks different from those of your unbelieving neighbors, family members, and friends. Then reflect on how your life looks very much like theirs, even at points where you know it shouldn't because of your identity in Christ. Write down a few notes on the reasons for the similarities:

Pray

Heavenly Father, as I study your word in Leviticus, I pray you would create in me a desire to be set apart from the world in your holiness through Jesus and to be identified as a follower of Jesus, in whose name I pray. Amen.

Read

- Read Leviticus 11, which concerns laws requiring Israel to distinguish between ritually pure and impure animals in terms of diet, handling, and other matters.
- In the commentary, read "Context" (163-165), and section 4.f (44-49).
- Read Leviticus 11 again.

A. Making Distinctions Between Pure and Impure—Review "Context" (164) and Lev. 11:46-47. To understand Leviticus 11, it is important to note that every culture has its own way of dividing the animal world (for example, by habitat, diet, etc.). The ancient Israelites also divided the animal world in various ways, two of which are found in Leviticus 11.

1. What two questions do these divisions answer?

2. What two kinds of animals are addressed by the second division?

3. What is the law's purpose, according to Lev. 11:47?

B. Distinction Among Animals the Israelites Could Eat and Were Not to Eat—Read "Comment" on Lev. 11:2b-23 (165-169). This section of Leviticus 11 concerns distinctions Israelites were to make between the kinds of animals that were ritually impure and were not to be eaten and those that were ritually pure and could be eaten.

1. Earlier chapters in Leviticus about animal food offerings demonstrate that various herd and flock animals, such as cattle, sheep and goats, were ritually pure for Israelites to eat. What two requirements for edible land animals did these herd and flock animals meet?

2. Leviticus 11:4-8 specifies four examples of land animals that did not meet the purity requirements. The Israelites were not to eat or touch the carcasses of these animals (v. 8). But this prohibition was not absolute, since Lev. 11:24-26 allows that touching their carcasses would sometimes occur. What, then, did the prohibition of Lev. 11:8 mean concerning touching of these ritually impure animals?

3. What did the restriction of this regulation to animal carcasses imply about living animals?

4. Commentators have suggested a number of rationales for the division of land animals in Lev. 11:1-8, including four mentioned in the commentary (166-168). Briefly describe one reason why each of these views is problematic:

   • Hygienic explanations:

   • Cultic explanations:

   • Moral-symbolic explanations:

   • Anthropological explanations:

5. The difficulties with these explanations indicate that none accounts for all the data. What other reason should lead us to consider each of these explanations as academic guesswork?

6. Leviticus 11:9-12 deals with ritually pure and impure marine animals. Why would the Israelites, living in the desert wilderness, have been familiar with marine animals?

7. Leviticus 11:13-19 provides a list of ritually impure birds that the Israelites were not to eat. Many on this list appear to be carnivorous. What is one possible explanation these carnivorous birds were considered ritually impure (see also bottom of 167)?

C. Dealing with Ritual Impurity from Contact with Carcasses—Read "Comment" on Lev. 11:24-40 (169-171). This section of Leviticus 11 concerns ritual impurity caused by contact with various animal carcasses and how it is to be addressed.

1. Why did an Israelite who came into contact with an impure land animal need to wait until evening to become ritually pure?

2. Leviticus 11:29-38 concerns treating various items that become ritually impure through contact with impure swarming land creatures. Certain items could be washed to restore ritual purity but others, such as clay pots, were to be destroyed. How were these regulations sensitive to the realities of daily life?

D. Detestability of Eating Swarming Land Creatures—Read "Comment" on Lev. 11:41-45 (171-172). These verses emphatically prohibit the Israelites from eating such creatures (for example, snakes, mice, caterpillars), saying they would not only become ritually impure but would make themselves detestable before the Lord (v. 43). The reason is simply stated: "Be holy because I the Lord am holy" (vv. 44b, 45b). Briefly state in your own words the relationship between the prohibition and the reason given for it:

APPLY

A. Setting Ourselves Apart as God's People—Read "Meaning" (172-173). One of the purposes of the laws of Leviticus 11 was to show the people of Israel how to set themselves apart from other cultures as the unique and redeemed people of God. They were to do this by obeying his holy commands, thereby acknowledging and reflecting the Lord's holiness to the watching world. The commands concerning ritual purity in their diets identified them as the Lord's unique people, underscored his holiness, and reminded them to seek moral purity—not just ritual purity—in all of life. **Give one or two examples of how your obedience to the Lord's commands in the New Testament age might serve to identify or set you apart as a follower of Jesus:**

B. Reminders to Practice Moral Purity—As we've seen, the laws of Leviticus 11 concerning ritual purity—dietary restrictions, contamination from dead animals, cleaning rituals—were intended to continually remind the Israelites to pursue not only ritual purity in all of life, but *moral* purity as well ("Meaning," 173).

1. In Heb. 5:11-14, the author rebukes some of his listeners for becoming "dull of hearing" and ignoring their discipleship under God's Word. He admonishes them toward having "their powers of discernment trained by constant practice to distinguish good from evil" (ESV). Briefly explain how this admonition reflects the same purpose as the ritual purity laws of Leviticus 11:

2. Describe two or three areas of life in our contemporary culture where the principles of Leviticus 11 and Heb 5:11-14 require believers to be constantly diligent to distinguish between holiness and unrighteousness, between good and evil?

RESPOND

Meditate—In Phil. 4:8-9, the apostle Paul exhorts us to practice distinguishing the true from the false, the honorable from the dishonorable, the pure from the impure, and so forth, by "thinking on" the holy and good things he lists in this passage. Use Phil. 4:8-9 as your meditation this week, recognizing that the Lord continues to command us—as he did the Israelites in Leviticus 11—to set apart the holy from the ordinary in our lives.

Take Action—Think about the aspects of your weekly life that you intentionally pursue, or might choose to pursue, that set you apart from the world and identify you as a follower of Jesus. Write down a few things you feel are most critical to being "set apart" at this point in your life. Make a short, practical plan to pursue these each week going forward.

Laws on Pure and Impure Creatures, and How Israel is to Relate to Them

ANALYZE

Opening Prayer

Heavenly Father, as we study your word in Leviticus, we pray you would create in us a desire to be set apart from the world in your holiness through Jesus and to be identified as a follower of Jesus, in whose name we pray. Amen.

Share Reflections | 5 min.

Have each person share one reflection from the Reflect exercise on the first page of the Individual Study. You can do this in pairs, or in the larger group if you have time. This is not a time to critique or ask lots of questions of each other, but simply to share something God has put on your heart.

Clarify Issues from the Lesson | 10 min.

Back in the larger group, prepare for your discussion by clarifying any uncertainties about the Scripture or commentary, but be careful with your time. The purpose here is to focus on a few issues that may be particularly difficult, not to open a broad discussion about the lesson.

Meaning of Leviticus for Today | 20 min.

Take turns reading aloud each point below, and discuss the questions as a group:

A. Setting Ourselves Apart to the Lord—The laws of Leviticus 11 concerning *ritual* purity in terms of diet, dealing with animal carcasses, and cleansing continually reminded the Israelites to also pursue *moral* purity in their daily lives as a people set apart as holy and to reflect the holiness of their covenant King to the surrounding cultures. In 2 Tim. 2:21, Paul says, "If anyone cleanses himself from what is dishonorable, he will be a vessel for honorable use, set apart as holy, useful to the master of the house, ready for every good work." **Discuss some practical things we can do in our daily lives as followers of Christ that might serve as constant "reminders" to pursue moral purity, cleanse ourselves from what is dishonorable, and thereby set ourselves apart as holy and useful to the Lord:**

B. Identified as the Lord's Holy People—In Leviticus 11, the Israelite's special diet of ritually pure animals, in particular, set them apart from surrounding nations and identified them as followers of the one true God. Identify four or five "markers" of mature Christians that ought to characterize the public identities of Jesus' followers today. **Discuss ways each of these markers might be proclaimed to "the watching world" in real-life situations you may face during your ordinary interactions with others:**

CREATE

Physical Reminders to Practice Moral Purity | 20 min.

The Lord often provides his people with physical symbols and reminders of deeper spiritual realities. Scripture abounds with examples. Circumcision was a physical sign and reminder of the spiritual reality of the covenant between God and his people (Gen. 17:10-14; Rom. 2:28-29). Water baptism is a physical symbol and reminder of the spiritual reality that we have died and been raised to life with and in Christ (Rom. 6:4; Col. 2:12). The Lord's Supper is a physical symbol and reminder of Jesus' sacrifice on our behalf and the new covenant in his blood between God and his people (Mt. 26:26-28; Mk. 14:22-24; Lk. 22:19-20). Likewise, the laws of ritual purity of Leviticus 11 served as physical symbols and reminders to the Israelites that they were to pursue moral purity in their daily lives ("Comment," 173). **Discuss some "physical symbols" your church might use to remind its members of their calling to pursue holiness in the Lord. Be sure to discuss how a church might implement such reminders while guarding against the dangers of moralism that Paul emphasizes in Col. 2:20-23.**[1]

---

[1] "Since you died with Christ to the elemental spiritual forces of this world, why, as though you still belonged to the world, do you submit to its rules: 'Do not handle! Do not taste! Do not touch!'? These rules, which have to do with things that are all destined to perish with use, are based on merely human commands and teachings. Such regulations indeed have an appearance of wisdom, with their self-imposed worship, their false humility and their harsh treatment of the body, but they lack any value in restraining sensual indulgence" (NIV).

LAWS ON RITUAL IMPURITY THROUGH LOSS OF BLOOD IN CHILDBIRTH

Reflect

Have you ever felt unworthy to go to church and worship with others who seem to "have it all together"? Do you know anyone else who feels this way? On the other hand, have you had the sweet experience of feeling absolutely welcome and accepted in community despite struggling with sin or having weak faith? Take a few moments to write some reflections on your experiences:

Pray

Heavenly Father, as I study your word in Leviticus, I pray you would help me to understand both your passion for holiness and your desire for fellowship with your children who struggle to reflect your holiness. Thank you, in Jesus' name. Amen.

Read

- Read Leviticus 12, which begins a section of laws for ritual impurity arising from aspects of the human body (Leviticus 12-15). Specifically, Leviticus 12 concerns a new mother's ritual impurity in connection with blood loss in childbirth.
- In the commentary, read "Context" (173-174), and sections 5.a-b (55-62). Review section 4.f (44-49).
- Read Leviticus 12 again.

UNDERSTAND

A. The Lord's Accommodation of Israel's Cultural Realities—Review "Introduction," section 5.a (55-57). Leviticus provides an example of the concept of "accommodation," meaning that the Lord communicates his values to us in ways we can understand by using the cultural realities that already exist in our society. While the idea of ritual purity may seem foreign to many moderns, the system was an understood reality in ancient Near Eastern cultures, including Israel (see 44-45), and included the concept that childbirth made the mother ritually impure. It therefore makes sense that the Lord used this system to teach his people about his character and his desires for them. While the rationale behind it is not stated, the Lord's *purpose* in using it is clear: He wanted the Israelites to understand that he is completely pure and holy and that they were to reflect his purity and holiness by making distinctions not only in the ritual realm, but also in the moral realm (see further pp. 48-49).

B. Ritual Impurity from Birth of a Son—Review "Context" (173-174) and read "Comment" on Lev. 12:1-4 (174-177). Leviticus 12 describes a three-stage purification process for a woman who has just given birth. The text is clear that her ritual impurity is not because of the child's birth—an event of great joy in Israel (Gen. 33:5; Ps. 127:3)—but because of blood loss during and after childbirth.

1. Identify the three stages of the purification process:

2. Since performing an action three times was a way of underscoring or emphasizing it (cf. 1 Sam. 20:41; 1 Kgs. 17:21), what purpose might this three-stage process have served?

3. Leviticus does not explain whether Israel had a specific rationale for why blood loss in childbirth caused ritual impurity. Whatever the rationale, if any, Israel had a positive view of children and childbirth. Briefly describe the three Scriptures cited in the commentary (175) for this view:

4. The first stage of a new mother's purification lasted seven days (Lev. 12:2), a number associated with completeness and thoroughness (cf. Lev. 26:18, 21). What was the purpose of this waiting period?

5. How is the new mother's impurity similar to that of her monthly period? Did this cause a woman to be totally isolated? What was a possible benefit of these laws?

6. In the case of the birth of a son, the boy would be circumcised on the eighth day. What was the reason for this?

7. The mother's second stage of purification also began on this eighth day after a son's birth. What two specific prohibitions did this stage entail?

C. Ritual Impurity from Birth of a Daughter—Read "Comment" on Lev. 12:5 (177-179). Leviticus 12:5 concerns provisions for ritual purification for blood loss during the birth of a daughter.

1. What significant difference between provisions made for a daughter's birth and those made for a son's does the commentary first address? Why was this difference a great mercy?

2. Although the daughter was not circumcised, this did not mean she was not a member of the covenant community. Why not?

3. What is the second significant difference the commentary discusses between provisions made for a daughter's birth and those made for a son's?

4. Some commentators have suggested that the differences are based on sexist values. Briefly describe two reasons this is unlikely:

D. Final Purification Process for Loss of Blood in Childbirth—Read "Comment" on Lev. 12:6-8 (179-180). A new mother's impurity in childbirth was considered a "major" impurity and thus required her to bring sacrifices to complete her purification. This final stage of purification was the same regardless of whether the child was a boy or a girl. Leviticus 12:6-8 specifies two sacrifices: the purification offering and a burnt offering.

1. What purpose did the purification offering serve in this context?

2. What dual role did the burnt offering likely serve in this context?

3. If the new mother was unable to afford a lamb for the burnt offering, she could bring a turtle dove or pigeon instead, and one of those birds for the purification offering as well. What did this merciful concession demonstrate and anticipate on the Lord's part?

APPLY

A. Laws of Ritual Purity as Reminders To Worship and Fellowship—Read "Meaning" (180). A new mother's ritual impurity meant she could not go to the tabernacle or partake of fellowship meals (see Lev. 15:31; 7:19-20). But Leviticus 12 makes clear that the Lord provided for her purification so she could again participate fully in Israel's covenant worship. Both parts of the law served as reminders. First, it reminded the Israelites of the Lord's blazing holiness: Only the ritually pure could draw near to his dwelling. Second, it reminded them of the Lord's intention for humanity since the beginning: to come before him in worship and celebrate fellowship with him and one another (180). **Reflect for a few minutes on whether you have any reminders in your own life of the Lord's holiness and his desire for his followers to worship him and fellowship with one another. Write a few notes below about those reminders, if you have them, or about some reminders you might incorporate into your life to serve these purposes:**

B. Importance of Being Connected in Community—The Lord provided a process, witnessed by the community, by which a new mother was purified after childbirth and restored to participating in worship and fellowship meals. This served as vivid picture for Israel of the value and importance of being connected in community. The New Testament carries forward this value. **Describe briefly in your own words how Heb 10:24-25 reflects the Lord's values in Leviticus 12 for being connected to the covenant community.**

RESPOND

Meditate—Meditate this week on Paul's greeting in 2 Cor. 13:11-14 and how it reflects the Lord's intention in Leviticus 12 for his followers to come together to worship him and celebrate fellowship with him and one another. Ask the Lord to remind and help you pray for any relationships among your family, friends, co-workers, or church community that may need restoration, comfort, agreement, and peace, so you can together and celebrate fellowship with the Lord.

Take Action—As you reflect on those relationships, write down a few practical steps you can take to participate in the restoration, comfort, agreement, and peace for which you're praying. Begin taking some of those steps this week.

LAWS ON RITUAL IMPURITY THROUGH LOSS OF BLOOD IN CHILDBIRTH

ENGAGE

Opening Prayer

Heavenly Father, as we study your word in Leviticus, we pray you would help us to understand both your passion for holiness and your desire for fellowship with your children who struggle to reflect your holiness. Thank you, in Jesus' name. Amen.

Share Reflections | 5 min.

Have each person share one reflection from the Reflect exercise on the first page of the Individual Study. You can do this in pairs, or in the larger group if you have time. This is not a time to critique or ask lots of questions of each other, but simply to share something God has put on your heart.

Clarify Issues from the Lesson | 10 min.

Back in the larger group, prepare for your discussion by clarifying any uncertainties about the Scripture or commentary, but be careful with your time. The purpose here is to focus on a few issues that may be particularly difficult, not to open a broad discussion about the lesson.

Meaning of Leviticus for Today | 20 min.

Take turns reading aloud each point below, and discuss the questions as a group:

A. Rationale for Levitical Laws—As we've seen, the *rationale* for a law and its *purposes* are two different things. While the rationale behind the purity system is not stated, the Lord's *purpose* in using it is clear: He wanted Israel to understand he is completely pure and holy and that they were to reflect his purity and holiness by making distinctions not only in the ritual realm, but also in the moral realm (see further pp. 48-49). In a similar way, while God does not always tell us the rationale behind every biblical command, he does make his overall purpose clear: His commands are meant to guide us in good and upright paths (Ps 119:105) that we might spread his kingdom of goodness, justice, mercy, and love in the world (Eph 1:4; 2:10). The secular worldview of "questioning authority" is prominent in our modern Western society. As such, it also influences the Church and its efforts in discipleship and growing the covenant community to maturity in Christ. **Identify three or four areas of biblical teaching that may be particularly susceptible to questioning God's *rationale* as opposed to his *purposes*, and discuss how this might impact discipleship in the local church:**

B. Importance of Being Connected in Community—The Lord provided a process, witnessed by the community, by which a new mother was purified after childbirth and restored to participating in worship and fellowship meals. This served as vivid picture for Israel of the value and importance of being connected in community. Connecting people in community includes restoring and encouraging those who may be struggling with sin or faltering in their faith in some other way. **Read Rom. 15:1-7, and discuss three or four practical ways a church might follow Paul's instructions to help its members be connected, restored, and encouraged in community:**

EVALUATE

Caring for Those Away from Community | 20 min.

As we saw in our study of Leviticus 12, the laws for ritual purification of a new mother gave her a socially acceptable way of withdrawing from others to rest and recuperate. They also assumed her family members and friends could extend comfort to her during the time of her purification away from the larger community (176). In a similar way today, for reasons other than ritual or even moral impurity, members of your faith community may not be able to participate for a season in the community's worship or other fellowship because of illness, grief, caring for homebound family members, difficult work schedules, or other significant reasons. **Discuss some practical steps your church or small group might take to provide comfort, love, fellowship, encouragement, prayer, confession, hospitality and other forms of care for those who are away from community for a time (2 Cor. 13:11-14: Heb. 10:24-25; Jas. 1:27; 5:14-16; 1 Pet. 4:8-10).**

LAWS ON THE RITUAL STATUS AND TREATMENT OF SKIN DISEASES AND INFESTATIONS OF GARMENTS AND HOMES

ENGAGE

Reflect

If you consider yourself part of a faith community that claims to follow Jesus, you have leaders called to care for your community in many ways. This includes watching for and disciplining unrepentant immorality so it doesn't spread in the community. Write some reflections on how you feel about this kind of authority, especially if it were brought to bear on an area in your own life that your leaders believed involved disobedience to Jesus.

Pray

Heavenly Father, as I study your word in Leviticus, I pray you would help me gain a deeper appreciation for your holiness, your desire for our flourishing as your people, and the many ways unrepentant sin can spread in our community and destroy that flourishing. In Jesus' name I pray. Amen.

Read

- Read Leviticus 13-14, which continues a section of laws for ritual impurity arising from aspects of the human body (Leviticus 12-15). Specifically, Leviticus 13-14 concerns ritual impurity arising from various skin conditions and related infestations of garments and homes.
- In the commentary, read "Context" (181-182).
- Read Leviticus 13-14 again, if you have time. The Bible and commentary readings for this lesson are a bit longer than most lessons, so plan your time accordingly.

A. Ritual Impurity and Healing of Various Skin Conditions—Review "Context" (181-182), and read "Comment" on Lev. 13:1-46 (182-184) and vv. 45-46 (187-188). The ritual impurity addressed in Leviticus 13-14 results from something called *sara'at*. In humans, *sara'at* manifested itself in various types of skin afflictions and has traditionally, though wrongly, been translated "leprosy." In Leviticus 13-14, it refers not only to human skin conditions but also to infestations of garments (13:47-59) and homes (14:33-57).

1.   What were three common signs or indications of *sara'at*?

2.   Every case of an infection or infestation of *sara'at* resulted in severe ritual impurity, whether in humans, garments, or homes. What could it ultimately defile if left unchecked in Israel?

3.   Leviticus 13-14 is divided into five sections. Briefly describe the subject of each:

13:1-46:

13:47-59:

14:1-32:

14:33-53:

14:54-57:

4.   The first major section, Lev. 13:1-46, helped priests identify the presence of *sara'at* in humans. If the diagnosis was conclusive either way, the priest would proclaim the person impure or pure. What happened if the diagnosis wasn't conclusive?

5. Many commentators believe *sara'at* does not refer simply or perhaps at all to "leprosy," but to a range of skin conditions or diseases. The commentary prefers the translation, "ritually defiling skin disease." What benefits does this translation have?

6. The ritually defiling skin diseases of *sara'at* resulted in major ritual impurity. Since major impurities spread easily by physical contact, the law focused on minimizing contact between those with and without the impurity. This also minimized spread of any *sara'at* infections that were contagious. Briefly describe the three rules that those with *sara'at* were required to follow:

B. Becoming Ritually Pure After a Defiling Skin Disease—Read "Comment" on Lev. 14:1-32 (190-194). Those with *sara'at* would undoubtedly have prayed to the Lord for healing (Num. 12:11-13; cf. Lk. 5:12-13). After being healed, they then needed to remove the ritual impurity caused by the *sara'at*.

1. The process to become ritually pure was gradual and involved three ceremonies corresponding to three different degrees of purity. What was the ritual state of a person after each of these ceremonies?

2. Once the priest pronounced someone ritually pure in the first ceremony, they would release a live bird into the open fields. This act parallels the release of a live goat in Lev. 16:21-22. What does this parallel suggest about the live bird?

3. After the final ceremony, the person being purified was now in a regular state of purity and could fully participate in the covenant community. What three atoning sacrifices did this final ceremony entail?

C. Ritual Impurity and Treatment of Garments and Homes—Read "Comment" on Lev. 13:47-59 (189-190) and 14:33-53 (195-197). Since the same signs were often present for human skin conditions and for fungal infestations of garments or homes, Hebrew speakers used the term *sara'at* in both cases.

1. If a garment infestation was deemed persistent or malignant, what did the law require, and why would this have been a significant consequence to the Israelites?

2. The law for ritual impurity of a home infection applied in the land of Canaan, where the Lord was sending Israel and where they would dwell in permanent houses rather than in tents. Leviticus 14:34 says the Lord might at times put a ritually defiling infestation in a house. Why does this statement not mean he was punishing someone for sin?

3. Why would the priest command a suspicious home to be emptied before he examined it for a defiling infestation, and why was this a gracious provision from the Lord?

4. If the infestation was found to have spread on the walls of a house after a seven-day quarantine, what happened to the impure building materials, and what purpose did that serve?

APPLY

A. Suffering as a Sign of Sin—Read "Meaning" (188-189). An Israelite quarantined for infection with *sara'at* might have been suffering discipline from the Lord for a specific sin and may very well have examined his or her life to see whether this was, in fact, the case (Psalm 38:3; 41:4; 103;3; 139:23-24). But nothing in Leviticus 13 assumes that *sara'at* or any other illness is the result of specific sin, and the Book of Job clearly demonstrates that suffering and sin are not always causally connected (cf. Job 1:8). **Describe how Jesus teaches this principle in Jn. 9:1-3:**

B. Costliness of Dealing with Moral Impurity—Read "Meaning" (197-198). Dealing with ritual impurity in ancient Israel often required God's people to undertake costly actions, including living outside the camp and community (Lev. 13:45-46), burning garments (Lev. 13:47-59), and tearing down their own homes (Lev. 14:43-45). Such costly actions would have taught them that the Lord was worthy of their deepest love and respect. It also would have reminded them of the love they were to show to their families and neighbors, since failing to deal properly with diseases or infestations could have caused great harm to the entire community. **Describe two or three situations today that would require a Christian to take costly action to properly deal with their own sin or other moral weakness in order to love their families or community:**

RESPOND

Meditate—Leviticus 13 aimed to minimize the spread of ritual impurity in the community. But the laws for dealing with *sara'at* also served to minimize the spread of potentially contagious diseases. This illustrates an important principle about God's created order: His creation is both moral and physical, and his commands are intended to help us flourish both morally and physically. Meditate this week on the Ten Commandments in Exodus 20:1-17, and reflect on how each of these moral commands helps us to flourish physically as God's beloved children.

Take Action—As you reflect this week on the Ten Commandments, pay attention to the ways in which your and others' moral or immoral actions—in thought, word, or deed—have direct or indirect implications in the physical realm, for good or for bad. Make notes on what you observe, and bring your observations to the Lord as you seek his wisdom for living, his forgiveness for anything you should confess, and his mercy and grace for those in need of moral and physical flourishing.

Laws on the Ritual Status and Treatment of Skin Diseases and Infestations of Garments and Homes

ANALYZE

Opening Prayer

Heavenly Father, as we study your word in Leviticus, we pray you would help us gain a deeper appreciation for your holiness, your desire for our flourishing as your people, and the many ways unrepentant sin can spread in our community and destroy that flourishing. In Jesus' name we pray. Amen.

Share Reflections | 5 min.

Have each person share one reflection from the Reflect exercise on the first page of the Individual Study. You can do this in pairs, or in the larger group if you have time. This is not a time to critique or ask lots of questions of each other, but simply to share something God has put on your heart.

Clarify Issues from the Lesson | 10 min.

Back in the larger group, prepare for your discussion by clarifying any uncertainties about the Scripture or commentary, but be careful with your time. The purpose here is to focus on a few issues that may be particularly difficult, not to open a broad discussion about the lesson.

Meaning of Leviticus for Today | 20 min.

Take turns reading aloud each point below, and discuss the questions as a group:

A. The Spread of Moral Impurity in the Community—The nature of *sara'at* in ancient Israel entailed sickness and damage below the surface of the skin and of building materials (Lev. 13:3; 14:37) and the tendency of the disease or infestation to spread (Lev. 13:7, 51; 14:43-44). The nature of this *ritual* impurity was an illustration to Israel, as it is for us, of the nature of *moral* impurity, which tends to operate beneath the surface and spreads to other people, communities, and even the creation itself (Rom. 5:12; 8:20-22). **Using three or four examples of moral impurities in our culture—including in the Church—diagnose the ways that each tends to be hidden "beneath the surface" and spreads to others:**

B. Protecting the Community from Others' Sin—The laws of Leviticus 13 sometimes required individuals to live outside the camp, and thus outside the community of Israel (see Lev. 13:46). These rules weren't meant to increase the hardship such individuals were already experiencing; they were meant to prevent the spread of potentially infectious disease and to prevent impurity from spreading throughout the community and defiling the Lord's holy dwelling (188). The New Testament demonstrates this principle in the realm of moral rather than ritual purity. In 1 Cor. 5:11, Paul instructs the Corinthian church in the practice we call "excommunication" today, commanding them "not to associate with anyone who bears the name of brother if he is guilty of sexual immorality or greed, or is an idolater, reviler, drunkard, or swindler—not even to eat with such a one" (ESV). Paul states the rationale in v. 6: "Do you not know that a little yeast spreads through the whole lump of dough?" Yet in his second letter to the Corinthians, he admonishes them to forgive the man they have excommunicated (implying that he had since repented), and to comfort and reaffirm their love for him (2 Cor. 2:5-8). Spend some time sharing your feelings about Paul's instructions in these two letters, including the list of moral impurities in 1 Cor. 5:11 and how we tend to react to these today in community. **Discuss three or four practical ways your church or small group might attempt to follow these New Testament commands that would honor the principles they express:**

EVALUATE

Leaders Diagnosing and Disciplining Sin | 20 min.

Throughout Leviticus 13-14, the Lord commands the priests to administer these laws of examining, diagnosing, quarantining, and purifying ritual and physical impurity in the community of Israel. This demonstrates an important aspect of the Lord's provision for our flourishing: He gives us human leaders to help administer his laws to us and calls us to submit to their authority (Tit. 1:5-9; Heb. 13:17; 1 Pet. 5:2-5). The New Testament makes clear that our leaders are charged with identifying sin in the community, calling it out, and administering discipline where needed (2 Cor. 10:5-6; 1 Tim. 5:20; 2 Tim. 4:2; Tit. 1:9; 2:15). **Discuss candidly how you feel about these principles of submitting to the authority of your leaders, who diagnose and discipline sin in your community. Identify situations in which you might easily submit to their decisions and others in which you might find this more difficult.**

FURTHER LAWS ON RITUALLY DEFILING BODY FLUIDS

ENGAGE

Reflect

Spend some time thinking of situations in your own experience, or perhaps in contemporary culture, where someone doing wrong has emboldened, encouraged, enticed, or incited others to the same wrong. These examples don't need to be of horrendous evils but can simply be the sins of our ordinary, daily lives. Write a few reflections on why you think our fallen human nature is so susceptible to the "contagion of sin".

Pray

Heavenly Father, as I study your word in Leviticus, I pray that you would warn me by your Spirit of the contagious nature of sin, convict me of my own unrepented sin, and encourage me with the knowledge that you have forgiven my sin and redeemed me by the blood of Christ, in whose name I pray. Amen.

Read

- Read Leviticus 15, which continues a section of laws for ritual impurity arising from aspects of the human body (Leviticus 12-15), specifically the voluntary and involuntary discharge of certain bodily fluids.
- In the commentary, read "Context" (198-199), and review "Introduction," section 5.b (57-62).
- Read Leviticus 15 again.

UNDERSTAND

A. Ritual Impurity from Male Bodily Discharges—Read the "Comment" on Lev. 15:1-18 (199-202). This section deals with two kinds of fluid discharges from a man's body. Lev. 15:2-15 concerns what we might call *abnormal* discharges, meaning they are not part of normal, healthy life. Lev. 15:16-18 concerns what we might call *normal* discharges, specifically the emission of semen. Both generally involved genital discharge and resulted in ritual impurity for the ancient Israelites.

1. This section involves unusual discharges that caused continual dripping or the obstruction of normal male discharge. What condition did both of these symptoms signify?

2. Male genital discharges in this section were considered major ritual impurities. What was one serious ramification of a major impurity?

3. The man with the discharge was not simply in need of ritual purification, but atonement. Why was this the case?

4. Leviticus 15:16-18 concerns normal male discharges, specifically of semen. Verses 16-17 appear to deal with a normal discharge other than during sex, such as a nocturnal emission, while verse 18 deals with sexual emissions. Both types were considered minor impurities that made the man unclean until evening, requiring him to wash his clothes and bathe. The Bible does not state the Israelite's rationale for sexual emissions causing impurity. What practical consideration have some commentators noted regarding a possible rationale?

5. In keeping with the Lord's perspective, the Israelites had positive views of sex (Prov. 5:15-19; Song of Songs) and childbirth (Gen. 1:28; 35:5; Ps. 127:3), both of which caused ritual impurity. This may seem strange to modern sensibilities, but we view certain activities that make us physically impure in the same way. List two or three such activities, other than the commentary's examples:

B. Ritual Impurity from Female Bodily Discharges—Read "Comment" on Lev. 15:19-30 (202-204). This section deals with both normal and abnormal fluid discharges from the female body. As with male bodily discharges, both resulted in ritual impurity for the ancient Israelites.

1. Leviticus 15:19-24 concerns normal discharges of a woman's menstrual flow. The purification rites in this case were more involved than for a man's normal discharges in vv. 16-18. This was not because men were treated more favorably. The same process was required for men and women for abnormal discharges. Lev. 15:13-15, 28-30. Why, then, the more complex purification rites for women's menstrual flows?

2. Significantly, the purification rites for a woman's normal menstrual flow did not involve offering sacrifices at the tent of meeting. What practical mercy did this provide?

3. Likewise, the law of Leviticus did not prohibit contact with menstruating women (though the contagious ritual impurity required normal purification by washing clothes and bathing). What two practical mercies did this provide the Israelites?

4. Leviticus 15:25-30 concerns abnormal female discharges, that is, not the normal flow of menstrual blood. These resulted in major impurity, just like a male's abnormal discharge, and required the same purification process (vv. 28-30). Describe what might cause this type of discharge, and list two examples:

C. Defiling the Lord's Holy Dwelling. Read "Comment" on Lev. 15:31-33 (204-205). Leviticus 15:31 is a concluding verse that concerns the reality that major impurities among the Israelites *automatically* defiled the Lord's dwelling place, the tent of meeting. Thus someone with a major impurity could defile the sanctuary without actually coming near it or intending to defile it. Because such ritual impurity was unintentional, sacrifice could atone for it. However, if the people didn't deal properly with their ritual impurity, the defilement would remain on the Lord's dwelling.

1. What additional risk did the Israelites run if they failed to deal properly with major ritual impurities, such as abnormal discharges of body fluids?

2. If Israelites failed to become ritually pure after an abnormal discharge and the impurity spread throughout the camp, further defiling the Lord's home, what would this entail beyond simply failing to acknowledge the Lord's holy kingship?

3. In Lev 15:31, the Lord exhorts Moses and Aaron to "keep the people of Israel separate from their impurity" (ESV translation). What did the Lord mean by this command? From what, in his mercy, was he warning the people to be "separated"?

APPLY

A. Purity in All Areas of Life—Read "Meaning" (205). Leviticus makes it clear that the Israelites were to deal properly with ritual impurity in all areas of life, such as the food they ate (Lev. 11), diseases and infestations (Lev. 13-14), and natural life processes, such as childbirth (Lev. 12) and sex (Lev. 15). And as we've seen, the laws of ritual purity were meant to teach Israel that they were to pursue moral purity in all areas of life to reflect the holy character and values of their covenant King. **Describe three or four areas in our lives today where the Lord would have us**

seek moral purity but where our culture—in the realms of business, entertainment, relationships, education, law, art, or others—dismisses the idea of moral purity, or may actively push against it.

B. Separated from Our Impurity—In Lev. 15:31, the Lord commands his people to be kept "separate from their uncleanness" (ESV). As the commentary explains, the Lord was warning the Israelites to separate themselves properly from their ritual impurity and so avoid the punishment associated with ongoing uncleanness that dishonored their holy King (204). **Read 1 Tim. 2:5-6 and 1 Pet. 1:17-19 and describe in your own words how the apostles say we are separated today from the consequences of our moral impurity and how we are to respond in light of this reality:**

RESPOND

Meditate—Meditate this week on 1 Pet. 1:17-19. Spend time thanking the Lord for his grace revealed in the passage and for his help obeying its command: "Since you call on a Father who judges each person's work impartially, live out your time as foreigners here in reverent fear. For you know that it was not with perishable things such as silver or gold that you were redeemed from the empty way of life handed down to you from your ancestors, but with the precious blood of Christ, a lamb without blemish or defect" (NIV).

Take Action—As you meditate on and pray 1 Pet. 1:17-19, note areas in your life where you might excel even more in living before the Lord in reverent respect for his holiness. Pick one of those areas, and take a few simple steps this week to increasingly pursue reverent respect for the Lord.

FURTHER LAWS ON RITUALLY DEFILING BODY FLUIDS

ANALYZE

Opening Prayer

Heavenly Father, as we study your word in Leviticus, we pray you would warn us by your Spirit of the contagious nature of sin, convict us of our own unrepented sin, and encourage us with the knowledge that you have forgiven our sin and redeemed us by the blood of Christ, in whose name we pray. Amen.

Share Reflections | 5 min.

Have each person share one reflection from the Reflect exercise on the first page of the Individual Study. You can do this in pairs, or in the larger group if you have time. This is not a time to critique or ask lots of questions of each other, but simply to share something God has put on your heart.

Clarify Issues from the Lesson | 10 min.

Back in the larger group, prepare for your discussion by clarifying any uncertainties about the Scripture or commentary, but be careful with your time. The purpose here is to focus on a few issues that may be particularly difficult, not to open a broad discussion about the lesson.

Meaning of Leviticus for Today | 20 min.

Take turns reading aloud each point below, and discuss the questions as a group.

A. The Contagion of Moral Impurity—The law of Leviticus 15 was intended to prevent ritual impurity from spreading through the community of Israel and defiling the Lord's holy dwelling place, the tent of meeting. As we've seen, the Lord intended the ritual purity laws of Leviticus to teach Israel—and to teach us today—about moral purity. We are now the dwelling place of the Holy Spirit of God (1 Cor. 6:19). **Identify three or four situations in which one person's moral impurity can spread to others, defiling the dwelling place of the Holy Spirit across a community, and diagnose how the moral impurity spreads in each situation:**

B. Experiencing the Lord's Discipline for Moral Impurity—Those of us who believe and have been redeemed by the blood of Christ have received "forgiveness of our trespasses, according to the riches of his grace" (Eph. 1:7). However, the Lord may discipline us for our sin (Heb. 12:5-11). **Read 1 Cor 11:17-34. Give four or five principles that can be gleaned from the text regarding moral impurity and the Lord's discipline.** Issues to explore might include: What examples of moral impurity does the text describe? What are some characteristics of moral impurity? How does moral impurity enter a community? What is the relationship between moral impurity and the Lord's holiness? How are we to guard against moral impurity? What may be some consequences of moral impurity?

EVALUATE

Purifying Ourselves in the World | 20 min.

The laws of Leviticus are clear that the Israelites could become ritually impure as they engaged in ordinary activities of life that were considered good and blessed by the Lord, such as childbirth (Lev. 12) and sex (Lev. 15). In the same way today, we can become morally impure as we engage in ordinary and good activities and relationships, even as we pursue things that may be approved by God. **Spend some time evaluating how this can be the case in various aspects of our lives, and what we might do to avoid entanglement with moral impurity (Heb. 12:1) as we pursue holiness because the Lord himself is holy (1 Pet. 1:15):**

LEVITICUS 16

THE DAY OF ATONEMENT

ENGAGE

Reflect

Write down a few reflections below on these aspects of your relationship with the Lord: When you come before him, how confident do you feel of his acceptance of you and desire for fellowship through his Son, Jesus? What are some of the factors that affect the degree of your confidence? To what extent do you experience the lifting of guilt because of the Lord's forgiveness? In what ways do you experience it emotionally, spiritually, physically or otherwise?

Pray

Heavenly Father, as I study your word in Leviticus, I pray you would help me to know the reality that you have cleansed me and forgiven my sins through the blood of your Son, Jesus Christ, and to experience the lifting of the guilt from my heart through Jesus, in whose name I pray. Amen.

Read

- Read Leviticus 16, which established the Day of Atonement for the people of Israel. This special day of sacrifice, purification, and worship atoned once each year for the Israelites' unaddressed sins and impurity so they could continue in covenant fellowship with their Holy King.
- In the commentary, read "Context" (206-207). You may also want to review the material on atonement in the "Introduction", section 4.g (50-54).
- Read Leviticus 16 again.

A. Entering the Most Holy Place—Read the "Comment" on Lev. 16:1-10 (207-210). This section of Leviticus 16 concerns the directions, animals, clothing, and rituals necessary for the High Priest to enter the Most Holy Place to begin the ceremony of the Day of Atonement.

1. The Lord's instructions to Moses were clear that Aaron, the High Priest, was not to come into the Most Holy Place whenever he chose. What are three reasons the commentary identifies for this strong warning (208)?

2. The Lord instructed Aaron not to wear his ornate, high-priestly garments into the Most Holy Place, but to wear a simpler set of plain, linen clothes. Although Leviticus 16 doesn't explicitly state the reason, what two possibilities does the commentary suggest?

3. Before putting on his simple, linen clothing, Aaron was required to ritually cleanse himself by washing his entire body, not just his hands and feet. What did this act of washing underscore?

B. Atoning for Sin Against the Lord's Kingly Rule—Read the "Comment" on Lev 16:11-28 (210-212). This section of Leviticus 16 concerns the purification offering Aaron was to make on behalf of himself and all the priests to cleanse the Lord's sanctuary from the defilement of their sins and ritual impurities.

1. Since the Israelites' sins and ritual impurities defiled the sanctuary, the initial rite in the Day of Atonement focused on cleansing the sanctuary's three important spaces. In what order was Aaron to cleanse these sacred spaces?

2. Upon entering the Most Holy Place, Aaron was to burn incense to create a cloud to conceal the atonement cover (some translations, "mercy seat"). What was the atonement cover (210)?

3. To cleanse the Most Holy Place, Aaron was to sprinkle blood from the bull of the purification offering on the atonement cover. What reasoning does the commentary give for why the atonement cover was the specific place atonement was to be made?

C. Removing Sin from the Midst of Israel. Read the "Comment" on Lev 16:20-22 (212-213). In the previous section, sin and ritual impurity were treated as a defiling substance that had to be cleansed from the Lord's sanctuary by the purification offering. In this section, sin is treated as a lethal substance that had to be removed from the camp of Israel by placing it on the head of the *azazel* goat, or "scapegoat."

1. Aaron began the rite by confessing all the Israelites' sins and placing them on the goat. Why did the rite of the "scapegoat" begin with confession?

2. Unlike the cleansing of the sanctuary, Aaron performed this rite publicly in view of the entire camp of Israel. What did the public rite of the "scapegoat" allow the Israelites to witness?

3. What three observations does the commentary give to support the conclusion that, as a consequence of this rite, the "scapegoat" bore not only the Israelites' sins, but also the penalty for their sins?

D. Properly Observing the Day of Atonement. Read the "Comment" on Lev 16:29-31 (214-215). This section of Leviticus 16 memorialized for the Israelites several key aspects of how they were to observe the Day of Atonement throughout their generations.

1. Briefly describe the three instructions in these verses for observing the Day of Atonement:

2. The Israelites' "humbling" themselves before the Lord no doubt entailed some sort of self-denial, such as fasting. Self-denial was often an outward sign of a repentant heart. Why would a repentant heart be an important aspect of the rites in the Day of Atonement?

3. What was the purpose of the Day of Atonement being a day of complete Sabbath rest?

E. Jesus and the Day of Atonement. Read "Meaning" (215-216), Heb 9:11-14, 24-26; Isa 53:8, 11-12.

1. On the Day of Atonement, Aaron was to enter the Most Holy Place, the Lord's earthly throne room, with the sacrificial blood of a bull. How does Heb 9:11-14 contrast this with Jesus' role as our perfect high priest?

2. Likewise, Aaron and the high priests after him were to enter the Most Holy Place once a year to offer not their own blood, but the blood of bulls, to atone for Israel's sin. How does Heb 9:24-26 contrast this with Jesus' role as our perfect high priest?

3. The "scapegoat" bore on itself the sins of Israel out of the camp and into the wilderness to a "land cut off" from the worshipping community (Lev 16:21-22; "Comment," 212-213). How does Isaiah (53:8, 11-12) describe the Lord's suffering servant (Jesus) in these same terms?

APPLY

A. Dealing Regularly with Our Sin—Leviticus 16 memorialized the Day of Atonement as a "statute forever" or "lasting ordinance" the Israelites were to observe every year from generation to generation (Lev 16:34; "Comment", 214-215). In other words, the rites of the Day of Atonement were to be regular and ongoing. The Day of Atonement dealt with all of Israel's sins that had gone unaddressed, whether unintentional sins of which they were unaware or intentional sins of rebellion (211). In the New Covenant age, we are no longer called to observe Day of Atonement rites because Jesus has fulfilled them once and for all (Heb 10:1-14). But the ordinance of the Day of Atonement—like all of Leviticus—reflects the unchanging character, values, and will of the Lord for his people for all generations. The Lord calls us in Christ to draw near to him in humility, confess and repent of our sins, walk in the light of his righteousness, and seek his cleansing (2 Cor 7:1, 9-10; 2 Tim 2:21; Heb 10:19-22; Jas 4:6-8; 1 Jn 1:7, 9). **What are some things you might do to help you as you continue to deal regularly and in an ongoing way with your sin, both unintentional and rebellious?**

B. Sabbath Rest and a Repentant Heart—The Day of Atonement rites called the Israelites to humble themselves before the Lord with repentant hearts because the rituals mattered little if they did not acknowledge and turn from their sins (214). Likewise, it was a day of complete Sabbath rest, underscoring its holiness and allowing space for a focused time of prayer and petition to the Lord (214). Clearly the Lord connects our need for Sabbath reflection with presenting ourselves humbly and repentant before him so we can deal rightly with our sin. **How might the Lord's desire for our Sabbath rest in the context of the Day of Atonement affect the ideas you noted in response to question A, above?**

Meditate—Meditate this week on Heb 10:19-23, especially as you spend time with the Lord in prayer: "Therefore, brothers and sisters, since we have confidence to enter the Most Holy Place by the blood of Jesus, by a new and living way opened for us through the curtain, that is, his body, and since we have a great priest over the house of God, let us draw near to God with a sincere heart and with the full assurance that faith brings, having our hearts sprinkled to cleanse us from a guilty conscience and having our bodies washed with pure water. Let us hold unswervingly to the hope we profess, for he who promised is faithful" (NIV).

Take Action—Aaron's confidence in entering the Most Holy Place depended on his following all the Lord's instructions so he would not die as his sons had when they entered the throne room without authorization (Lev 16:1-2; "Comment", 207-208). It also depended on the purification that came from offering the blood of the sacrificial bull (Lev 16:11, 14). As you meet with the Lord in prayer this week, be mindful of the confidence he has granted you to draw near to him with a sincere heart and to be cleansed by the blood of Jesus of any guilt you are bearing. Make it part of your prayers this week to thank him for opening the way into his throne room. Thank him for giving you confidence to draw near to him. Thank him for cleansing you from a guilty conscience. Thank him for purifying you through the sacrifice of his own blood (Tit 2:13-14; 1 Jn 3:3) to make you holy before him (Col 1:21-22; 1 Thess 3:11-13; 1 Pet 2:4-5, 9).

THE DAY OF ATONEMENT

— ANALYZE —

Opening Prayer

Heavenly Father, as we study your word in Leviticus, we pray you would help us to know the reality that you have cleansed us and forgiven our sins through the blood of your Son, Jesus Christ, and to experience the lifting of the guilt from our hearts through Jesus, in whose name we pray. Amen.

Share Reflections | 5 min.

Have each person share one reflection from the Reflect exercise on the first page of the Individual Study. You can do this in pairs, or in the larger group if you have time. This is not a time to critique or ask lots of questions of each other, but simply to share something God has put on your heart.

Clarify Issues from the Lesson | 10 min.

Back in the larger group, prepare for your discussion by clarifying any uncertainties about the Scripture or commentary, but be careful with your time. The purpose here is to focus on a few issues that may be particularly difficult, not to open a broad discussion about the lesson.

Meaning of Leviticus for Today | 20 min.

Take turns reading aloud each point below, and discuss the questions as a group:

A. Atoning for Sin Against the Lord's Kingly Rule—Aaron cleansed the Most Holy Place by sprinkling the blood of the purification offering on the atonement cover (some translations, "mercy seat") (Lev 16:14). The atonement cover rested on top of the ark of the covenant, which held the tablets of the law the Lord had given to Moses on Mt. Sinai (Ex 25:16, 21; 34:29). The Lord's presence dwelled above the atonement cover and from there, he met with Moses (Ex 25:22). The priests' sins were atoned for at this very place because it was the Lord's earthly throne: Their sins were rebellion against his kingly rule and defiled the very object that represented it (211). Now, in the New Covenant, the Lord calls us to draw near to him in the Most Holy Place in heaven with full confidence in the atoning sacrifice of Jesus' blood (Heb 9:19-23). But he calls us to do so with humble and repentant hearts (Jas 4:6-8), confessing our sins to him (1 Jn 1:7, 9). **Discuss some areas in our lives for**

which we need to confess and turn, where we tend to "dethrone" the Lord from his rightful, kingly rule and establish ourselves on the throne instead:

B. Lifting the Burden of Sin from Our Communities—The "scapegoat" of the Day of Atonement removed the guilt and burden of the Israelites' sins by virtue of the high priest placing their sins on its head and driving it from the camp into the wilderness, the "land cut off" (Lev 16:20-22; "Comment", 212-213). Jesus has now become both our great high priest (Heb 4:14) and the one who has borne all our sins away when he was "cut off out of the land of the living" for our sake (Isa 53:8, 11-12). Note also that the "scapegoat" rite was performed publicly, in full view of all the Israelites, so they could witness the goat bearing their sins into the wilderness, never to return (Ps 103:12; "Comment", 212). Its public nature was intended to lift the burden and guilt of sin from the Israelites' shoulders (213). **Discuss some practical ways your church, study group or other community might help lift the burden and guilt of sin from one another's shoulders by using reminders of what Jesus has done for us by cleansing us, removing our sin, and atoning for the guilt of our sin.** Be creative with these reminders: They might be verbal, visual, instructional, liturgical, sacramental, relational or any other kind of reminder.

CREATE

Entering with Confidence the Most Holy Place of Heaven | 20 min.

Hebrews 10:19-25 describes what Jesus has done for us as our great high priest and how the Lord calls us to respond. **Brainstorm in pairs or as a group a list of practical things you can do to respond to the exhortations of Heb 10:19-25.** Be sure to consider ideas that might help you individually and ideas to support others in your community. As with the exercise in B, above, be creative with the approaches and ideas you consider.

THE PROPER PLACE OF SACRIFICE AND PROPER USE OF ANIMALS' LIFEBLOOD

ENGAGE

Reflect

Write down a few reflections on daily cultural influences that challenge your allegiance to the Lord: What may tend to be "idols" or "false gods" in your life? Jesus said we cannot serve two "masters" (Mt 6:24). Are there other "masters" in your life besides him? If so, why do they have the potential power to command your allegiance or "worship"? What are the situations in which you find yourself tempted to serve them?

Pray

Heavenly Father, as I study your word in Leviticus, I pray you would help me identify each day the false "gods" of our culture that tempt me to worship them instead of you. Forgive me for failing to worship you as the only rightful God and Lord of my life. Thank you for providing a ransom for my sins of disloyalty in the sacrifice of your Son, Jesus, in whose name I pray. Amen.

Read

- Read Leviticus 17, which addresses the proper place of sacrifice for the Israelites, to keep them from sacrificing to false gods, and the proper use of an animal's blood, which was never to be consumed.
- In the commentary, read "Context" (217-218), and "Introduction," section 5.f (72).
- Read Leviticus 17 again.

A. Proper Place of Sacrifice for Israelites and Resident Aliens—Read the "Comments" on Lev. 17:3-7 and 8-9 (218-220). These two sections address the only proper place for an Israelite or resident alien to make a sacrificial animal offering—the Tent of Meeting (vv. 4, 5, 6)—and the only God to whom they were to make their offerings—the Lord himself (vv. 4, 5, 6).

1. Leviticus 17:7 provides context for the prohibition against killing sacrificial animals (such as oxen, lambs or goats) anywhere other than the Tent of Meeting. What practice were the Israelites engaging in that prompted this prohibition and warning from the Lord?

2. The commentary suggests an analogy between ancient Near Eastern polytheism and modern, Western materialism. How does this help explain why the Israelites were still engaging in false worship even after beginning to follow the Lord?

3. The Lord uses the metaphor of prostitution in v. 7 to describe the Israelites' continuing worship of demons, or false gods. Why was this a fitting metaphor?

4. Any Israelite (or resident alien, vv. 8-9) who violated this prohibition against sacrificing animals anywhere other than the Tent of Meeting was deemed guilty of bloodshed (v. 4b). Why?

5. Leviticus 17:8-9 extends the prohibitions on animal sacrifices to any resident alien living among the Israelites. Why do this and other laws for Israel address the participation of resident aliens in Israel's covenant worship?

6. The commentary identifies two effects of extending these laws for proper worship to Israel's resident aliens. What are they?

B. Prohibition Against Eating Blood—Read the "Comments" on Lev 17:10-12, 13-14 and 15-16 (220-223). These sections of Leviticus 17 concern prohibitions against eating the "lifeblood" of any animal, whether the animal was killed as a sacrifice, as a game animal in hunting, died of natural causes, or was killed by another animal.

1. Leviticus 17 does not explain why Israelites might have eaten raw, bloody meat or blood by itself and thus why the prohibition was necessary. What possibility does the commentary suggest?

2. Leviticus 17:11 gives the rationale for the prohibition against eating blood. Briefly describe the three related statements contained in this rationale (220-221):

3. The second statement in the rationale of Lev 17:11 gives two reasons why an animal's lifeblood must not be consumed. Briefly describe those two reasons:

4. The third statement in the rationale of Lev 17:11 explains that the animal's lifeblood was accepted as a ransom payment in place of the offeror's lifeblood. Briefly describe in your own words what this entailed:

5. The second clause in Lev 17:11 includes an extra "I" in the Hebrew text, so it reads literally, "and I myself have given [the animal's lifeblood] to you on the altar to make atonement for your lives." What about sacrifice does this emphasize?

6. Israelites and resident aliens could eat certain ritually pure animals (such as deer, quail and partridges) but could not use them for sacrifices. Therefore, their blood could not be placed on the altar and used for atonement. Instead, it was to be poured on the ground and covered with dirt. What two important goals did this requirement accomplish?

Read "Meaning" (223-224).

APPLY

A. Our Exclusive Relationship with the Lord—Leviticus 17 reminded the Israelites and any resident aliens living in the covenant community that their relationship with the Lord was exclusive, just as in the covenant of marriage (cf. Lev 17:7). As Jesus taught, "No one can serve two masters. Either you will hate the one and love the other, or you will be devoted to one and despise the other" (Mt 6:24). In the case of the ancient Israelites, the context was their continuing worship of demons, or false gods, as they came out of the polytheistic culture of Egypt. Most in the modern West are not in the habit of worshipping goat demons (v. 7), but "other masters" surround us (Mt 6:24). **Review the reflections you wrote at the beginning of this lesson and identify some things you can do to renew and strengthen your exclusive covenant relationship with the Lord and your worship of him:**

B. Respecting All Life as the Lord's—The prohibition against consuming blood in Leviticus 17 also reminded the Israelites to respect their covenant King by respecting that which belonged to him, namely, life itself. This served as a broader reminder to respect all life (not just animal life) because all life belongs to the Lord as its Creator and sovereign King. This responsibility to respect life is embodied in the Ten Commandments ("You shall not murder", Ex 20:13) and in various laws aimed at averting negligence that might harm or take human or animal life (e.g., Ex 21:29, 33-35; 22:10-14; Dt 22:8). **Reflect on and identify any areas in your life where your actions or failure to act might bring harm, injury or even death to another. Consider ways to remedy any of these areas where you may be failing to respect the Lord's sovereign ownership of others' lives (and perhaps your own):**

RESPOND

Meditate—Reflect this week on the reality depicted in Leviticus 17 that the Lord has graciously and mercifully exercised his sovereignty over all life, including yours, by providing a substitute for your "lifeblood," sending his Son to be the atoning sacrifice for your sins. Meditate this week on Mk 10:45, "For even the Son of Man did not come to be served, but to serve, and to give his life as a ransom for many" (NIV) and Rom 5:8-9, "But God demonstrates his own love for us in this: While we were still sinners, Christ died for us. Since we have now been justified by his blood, how much more shall we be saved from God's wrath through him!" (NIV).

Take Action—The law of Leviticus 17 prohibiting the consumption of an animal's lifeblood reminded the Israelites that all life belongs to the sovereign Lord and that he alone has the right to direct and use our lives for his purposes. While the immediate context for the ancient Israelites concerned the lifeblood of sacrificial animals, by extension the principle applies to all life, including our own. Paul makes it clear in 1 Cor 6:19-20 that we are not our own but have been bought for God with the price of his Son's own lifeblood. Reflect on the ways you are living before the Lord that respect his sovereignty over your life and then note some ways in which you might grow more deeply in that respect:

THE PROPER PLACE OF SACRIFICE AND PROPER USE OF ANIMALS' LIFEBLOOD

ANALYZE

Opening Prayer

Heavenly Father, as we study your word in Leviticus, we pray you would help us identify each day the false "gods" of our culture that tempt us to worship them instead of you. Forgive us for failing to worship you as the only rightful God and Lord of our lives. Thank you for providing a ransom for our sins of disloyalty in the sacrifice of your Son, Jesus, in whose name we pray. Amen.

Share Reflections | 5 min.

Have each person share one reflection from the Reflect exercise on the first page of the Individual Study. You can do this in pairs, or in the larger group if you have time. This is not a time to critique or ask lots of questions of each other, but simply to share something God has put on your heart.

Clarify Issues from the Lesson | 10 min.

Back in the larger group, prepare for your discussion by clarifying any uncertainties about the Scripture or commentary, but be careful with your time. The purpose here is to focus on a few issues that may be particularly difficult, not to open a broad discussion about the lesson.

Meaning of Leviticus for Today | 20 min.

Take turns reading aloud each point below, and discuss the questions as a group:

A. Respect for God's Creation—Leviticus 17 is clear that the blood of every animal is equated with its life and that the Lord is sovereign over all life; thus the Israelites were not free to use an animal's blood as they chose, but only as the Lord commanded (Lev 17:5-6, 10-4). These laws serve as a general reminder to respect all life, for all life belongs to the Lord, its Creator and King. For this reason, those who follow Jesus should be at the forefront of caring for life in all its forms: human (Lev 19:15-18), animal (Dt 5:14; Pr 12:10), and even plant life (Lev 25:2-5). This implies the necessity of caring for the environment, the larger structure of creation that supports all life. Indeed, one of God's original callings or vocations for humankind is that we cultivate and take care of his good creation (Gen 2:15). **Discuss some critical ways we as Christians should be at the forefront of respecting the**

Lord's sovereign right over all life forms on earth. Be sure to discuss some of the obstacles that may oppose this responsibility, even from within the Church itself:

B. Ensuring Proper Worship by the Entire Covenant Community—Leviticus 17 applied the laws for proper worship to foreigners, or resident aliens, who had come into the covenant community of Israel (Lev 17:8-9). Everyone in the community where the Lord himself dwelled was required to follow the laws of ritual purity and proper worship. These laws served at least two purposes: (1) avoiding syncretism of religious practices (that is, mixing pagan practices with Israel's, and therefore profaning the proper worship of God), and (2) welcoming those of other nations into the blessings of covenant relationship with the Lord (219-220). These principles for resident aliens, or new members of the covenant community, can be applied today to those in our communities who are either new church members, new believers, or perhaps "seekers" who do not yet know the Lord but are being drawn by him into belief. (For example, the apostle Paul warns against involving new believers too quickly in church leadership; 1 Tim 3:6.) **Discuss strategies, policies, and practical steps a church or Christian small group might take to welcome new believers and seekers into their community but also to safeguard the proper worship of the Lord, including the protection of correct doctrine (1 Tim 1:3; Tit 1:9):**

Proper Worship in the Midst of Cultural Idolatry | 20 min.

The context behind the first part of Leviticus 17 entailed the Israelites' continuing worship of false gods or demons (Lev 17:7), even after the Lord had delivered them out of Egypt. The Lord emphasized five times that there was only one proper place of worship, the Tent of Meeting, and only one god to be worshipped, the Lord himself (vv. 4a, 5, 6). He expressly stated, "This is so the Israelites will bring to the Lord the sacrifices they are now making in the open fields" (Lev 17:5a, NIV). In other words, some Israelites continued sacrificing to false gods or demons *apart from proper worship in the covenant community*. The writer of Hebrews echoes this concern when he warns against "giving up meeting together, as some are in the habit of doing" (Heb 10:25). Paul likewise admonishes us to proper worship of the Lord by not conforming ourselves to the patterns and practices of our culture (Rom 12:1-2). **Evaluate practical steps your church congregation or small group can take to help its members worship the Lord properly by encouraging engagement in the worshipping community and equipping them to resist idolatrous practices in the "open fields" of the surrounding culture:**

LEVITICUS 18

LAWS AGAINST CERTAIN SEX AND WORSHIP PRACTICES

ENGAGE

Reflect

Describe how you feel about God's commands in Scripture in terms of how they contribute or don't contribute to your enjoying life. Do his commands seem to help or hinder your living a worthwhile life? Do they help or hinder your living in ways that benefit others? What aspects of our culture might you enjoy more but feel constrained by God's law not to enjoy? Do any of your reflections raise issues you feel you should bring before the Lord for confession and for his help in shaping your heart to be more like his (Ps 51:10; Mt 5:8)?

Pray

Heavenly Father, as I study your word in Leviticus, help me see the beauty of your laws and commands for human life and flourishing. Shape my heart so that it yearns after righteousness on the earth as you do. I pray these things in the name of your Son, Jesus. Amen.

Read

- Read Leviticus 18, which addresses various sexual and worship practices forbidden to the Israelites. This chapter, along with Leviticus 19 and 20, form a unit of related laws that teach Israel how to live as the Lord's holy people in contexts beyond worship at the tabernacle.
- In the commentary, read the preface page (226) and "Context" (227-228).
- Read Leviticus 18 again.

A. Enjoying Life by Following the Lord Instead of the Culture—Read "Comments" on Lev. 18:1-5 (228-230). Leviticus 18, 19, and 20 form a "chiasm," a literary feature in a sort of sandwich pattern: A—B—A1. Chapters 18 (A) and 20 (A1) concern the Lord's commands for Israel to distinguish herself as holy by not imitating the surrounding nations, especially in worship and sexual practices, while ch. 19 (B) provides laws on a wide range of issues for Israel's holiness before the Lord (227). Leviticus 18 itself is also a chiasm, following a similar A—B—A1 pattern (227-228):

1. The opening verses, Lev. 18:1-5, comprise the first part of the chiasm. These verses accomplish three things. They first establish that Israel is to obey the Lord because he rescued them out of Egypt to be his very own. Describe the three related ideas about the Lord evoked here by the repeated phrase, "I am the Lord your God" (vv. 2, 4, 5):

2. Describe in your own words the second and third things these opening verses accomplish:

3. These opening verses admonish Israel not to follow certain sexual and worship practices of the surrounding nations of Egypt and Canaan. In v. 5, the Lord declares that a person who keeps his statutes and rules, rather than those of the nations, "shall live by them." What does this phrase mean?

4. The Lord's commands in these early verses remind Israel that he is the Creator God and has designed his world according to certain rules for the way life should be lived. The commentary likens his commands for life to the "borders of God's kingdom." What two things resulted as Israel stayed within these borders?

B. Illicit Worship and Illicit Sexual Relations—Read the "Comments" on Lev 18:6-23 (230-239). These sections of Leviticus 18 address three types of sins: sexual immorality, murder, and illicit worship practices, especially idolatry. The Bible identifies these sins as especially defiling for those who commit them and for the land on which they are committed:

1. Verses 6-17 deal with illicit sexual relations ("to uncover nakedness", ESV) with close relatives (whether close relatives by blood or by marriage). While ancient societies encouraged marriage within "clans" to some degree, they recognized there were appropriate boundaries that should not be crossed. Here the Lord himself provides the boundaries for Israel and makes it clear that crossing them defiles his people and the land. As vv. 6 and 14 explicitly state, an aspect of the prohibited conduct was a man "approaching" a closely related woman to have sex. What were two practical benefits of these laws?

2. The chart on page 232 of the commentary summarizes prohibited sexual relationships among close relatives addressed in Lev. 18:6-17. What are the five broad categories of women with whom an Israelite man was not to have sexual relations? [1]

3. The commentary explains that v. 18 is likely a prohibition against polygamy. Reasons that support this include use of the Hebrew phrase, "a woman in addition to her sister," which was a common expression not typically used for relatives. In any case, this prohibition was aimed at avoiding a particular situation. What was the situation and why was it to be avoided (p. 236)?

---

[1] Though these laws reference the man, they obviously were intended to prohibit women from the reciprocal roles in these relationships. Israel commonly framed laws using masculine singular terms, but it was generally understood that they applied to everyone in society. The Ten Commandments use a masculine singular throughout (the "you" in "you shall not kill" is masculine), but everyone knew these laws forbade both men *and women* from murder, adultery, stealing, etc.

4. Leviticus 18:20 prohibited a man from having sex with his neighbor's wife (and, of course, a woman from having sex with her neighbor's husband) because this would have been a common temptation in the camp of Israel. What two things does this prohibition not imply?

5. Leviticus 18:21 prohibited the Israelites from "offering" or dedicating their children to the demonic Canaanite god Molech (sometimes spelled "Molek"). What did it mean to offer children to Molech, and what additional offense against the Lord did this add to the idolatry of worshipping another god?

6. The Lord declared that worshipping Molech in this way would profane his name. What does it mean to profane the name of the Lord?

7. Leviticus 18:22 prohibits homosexual conduct between men (and by implication, between women) and refers to homosexual intercourse as "detestable" (NIV) or "an abomination" (ESV). The commentary notes two types of acts the Bible describes as detestable: One is considered detestable as a cultural matter and the other as a moral matter. Why is homosexual conduct considered detestable as a moral matter?

C. Avoiding God's Punishment by Keeping His Commands—Read "Comments" on Lev. 18:24-30 (239-240). The first section of the chiasm of Leviticus 18 (vv. 1-5), promised the Israelites a blessed life if they avoided the illicit practices of the surrounding nations. This last section of the chiasm (A1), mirrors the first by warning the Israelites that if they do not avoid those illicit practices, they may suffer the same punishments that the Lord intended to bring on the other nations.

1. Because the Canaanites had defiled themselves and the land with their detestable practices, the Lord was going to drive them from their land before the people of Israel. What metaphor does the Lord use to describe this punishment of the Canaanites?

2. To avert the same calamity for Israel, the Lord says he will "cut off" from Israel anyone who commits the detestable Canaanite practices he has prohibited. In what two ways could an Israelite be "cut off" from the people of God?

APPLY

Read "Meaning" (240-241).

A. The Marked Borders of God's Holy Kingdom—In Egypt, the Israelites had been in contact with a nation whose ways of life differed radically from the life the Lord intended for his creation, and the Israelites would experience the same again with the nations living in Canaan (v. 3). So this chapter begins and ends with the Lord's warning of the importance of obeying his commands. In effect, his commands marked out borders for his holy kingdom, within which his people could experience life under his blessing and favor (v. 5). In other words, God's commands are meant to align us with his intentions for this world so that we are not fighting against them (and thus, against the Lord), but rather can experience flourishing as God intends for his entire creation.

1. The Ten Commandments (Ex 20:1-17) are the Old Testament foundation of God's ethics for humanity, fully applicable today in the New Testament age. Review the ten commandments and write a short note on each one expressing how it enhances human flourishing:

2. At the end of Leviticus 18, the Lord makes it clear that he will oppose those who rebel against his commands (vv. 24-30). This is not only because it is an act of treason against him but also because it ignores and destroys the borders of his holy kingdom, which he has established for human flourishing. This understanding of the Lord's response to evil leads to a certain irony today. On the one hand, God's wrath against unrighteousness is sometimes viewed as the raging of a petty, angry deity. At the same time, when human leaders take action against things that destroy human flourishing—such as murder, theft, or human trafficking—they are often praised. What are some possible reasons for such different responses to God's actions against evil and man's actions against evil?

RESPOND

Meditate—Human flourishing is at its pinnacle when we are in right relationship with God. Following his commands does not earn us a standing of righteousness; that is the gift of God through faith in Jesus (Rom 5:9, 17; Eph 2:8-9). But Jesus is clear that keeping God's commands not only shows our love for him, it is also a means of his grace, love, and blessing to us. Reflect this week on his words in the Gospel of John: "If you keep my commands, you will remain in my love, just as I have kept my Father's commands and remain in his love" (Jn 15:10, NIV). "Whoever has my commands and keeps them is the one who loves me. The one who loves me will be loved by my Father, and I too will love them and show myself to them" (Jn 14:21, NIV).

Take Action—Print a copy of Mt 5:1-12 and keep it with you this week. As you have opportunities to live out even just one or two of the ethics reflected in Jesus' teaching, take notes on how your actions are contributing to human flourishing, both yours and others':

LAWS AGAINST CERTAIN SEX AND WORSHIP PRACTICES

ANALYZE

Opening Prayer

Heavenly Father, as we study your word in Leviticus, help us see the beauty of your laws and commands for human life and flourishing. Shape our hearts so that they yearn after righteousness on the earth as you do. We pray these things in the name of your Son, Jesus. Amen.

Share Reflections | 5 min.

Have each person share one reflection from the Reflect exercise on the first page of the Individual Study. You can do this in pairs, or in the larger group if you have time. This is not a time to critique or ask lots of questions of each other, but simply to share something God has put on your heart.

Clarify Issues from the Lesson | 10 min.

Back in the larger group, prepare for your discussion by clarifying any uncertainties about the Scripture or commentary, but be careful with your time. The purpose here is to focus on a few issues that may be particularly difficult, not to open a broad discussion about the lesson.

Meaning of Leviticus for Today | 20 min.

Take turns reading aloud each point below, and discuss the questions as a group:

A. Christian Ethics in Protecting the Sexually Vulnerable—The Lord has shown in Leviticus 18 his strong disapproval of sex acts, and even sexual advances, by the powerful against the vulnerable (vv. 6-17). Indeed, he has promised to bring his wrathful opposition against those who violate this ethic (vv. 24-29). As the Lord's ambassadors of reconciliation in the world (2 Cor 5:20), we are, above all, people called to bring his ethic into every area of life. Christians more than any others should be at the forefront of acting to protect the sexually vulnerable in all societies and cultures. **Discuss some critical ways we as individual Christians, and as local congregations and the universal Church, ought to be at the forefront of protecting the sexually vulnerable. Discuss some of the obstacles that may oppose the advancement of this ethic, even from within the Church.**

B. Ministering to Those with Same-Sex Attraction—As we've seen, the Lord in Leviticus 18 forbids homosexual conduct (v. 22). While some debate whether this prohibition has ongoing relevance today, it was noted that these prohibitions are in keeping with God's ethics for sex laid down in creation (Gen 1:27-28; 2:22-24), and that they are repeated in the New Testament as well (Rom 1:26-27; cf. Matt 19:4-5) (p. 238). This implies their ongoing relevance and means that certain types of relationships approved in many cultures today (such as same-sex marriage) are biblically out of bounds. There are many same-sex attracted Christians who agree with this and yet who also feel the Church is not a safe place to share their struggles—despite the fact we are called to "bear one another's burdens, and so fulfill the law of Christ" (Gal 6:2). **Discuss why the Church has not done a better job here and explore ways that we as individual Christians, local congregations, and small groups, might do a much better job of loving and supporting those in our midst with same-sex attraction. Focus especially on ways we can be *friend* and *family* for same-sex attracted people:**[2]

---

[2] "For a helpful approach to these questions, see Wesley Hill, *Spiritual Friendship: Finding Love in the Church as a Celibate Gay Christian* (Grand Rapids, MI: Brazos Press, 2015); Mark A. Yarhouse, *Homosexuality and the Christian: A Guide for Parents, Pastors and Friends* (Bloomington, MN: Bethany, 2010); *Understanding Sexual Identity: A Resource for Youth Ministry* (Grand Rapids, MI: Zondervan, 2013); Ed Shaw, *Same-Sex Attraction and the Church: The Surprising Plausibility of the Celibate Life* (Downers Grove, IL: InterVarsity Press, 2015). Wesley Hill has also written a short book describing his journey as a same-sex attracted Christian who is seeking to maintain biblical faithfulness (*Washed and Waiting: Reflections on Christian Faithfulness and Homosexuality* [Grand Rapids, MI: Zondervan, 2010])" (Sklar, *Leviticus* [Zondervan], forthcoming, at Lev 18:22, "Additional Note").

CREATE

Accountability in the Areas of Sexual Immorality and Improper Worship | 20 min.

Leviticus 18 focuses specifically on the illicit sexual and worship practices of the nations surrounding Israel. God warns his people not to practice these things that are morally detestable to him so that they do not defile his people and the land. In many ways, nothing has changed since the time of Moses. Sexual immorality and idolatry of all kinds run rampant in many cultures today, defiling the people who commit them and the places in which they are committed. In his first letter to the church in Corinth, the apostle Paul addresses both of these matters when he says to "flee from sexual immorality" (1 Cor 6:18) and "flee from idolatry" (1 Cor 10:14). In his personal instructions to Timothy, he notes that Christians are to flee from these temptations in the company of a faith community: "Flee youthful passions and pursue righteousness, faith, love, and peace along with those who call on the Lord from a pure heart" (2 Tim 2:22). **Discuss some practical ways your group might support one another in guarding against the sins of sexual immorality and the idolatries of our culture by pursuing righteousness, faith, love and peace together in community.**

THE LORD'S HOLY PRACTICES FOR HIS HOLY PEOPLE

ENGAGE

Reflect

Take time to reflect on your view of "holiness." What does holiness mean to you? Are you motivated to pursue personal holiness? If so, what motivates you? How do you evaluate personal holiness in yourself and others? Is the measure you use different for you than for others? If so, why? What place does the Lord's holiness play in your view or evaluation of your personal holiness?

Pray

Heavenly Father, as I study your word in Leviticus, deepen my appreciation for your holiness and your passion for mine. Help me see the connection between personal holiness and my obedience to your commands. And help me to become more like you, to be holy because you are holy. I pray these things in the name of your holy Son, Jesus. Amen.

Read

- Read Leviticus 19, which addresses the Lord's holy practices for his holy people. This chapter, along with Leviticus 18 and 20, form a unit of related laws that teach Israel how to live as the Lord's holy people in contexts beyond worship at the tabernacle.
- In the commentary, read "Context" (241-42).
- Read Leviticus 19 again.

UNDERSTAND

A. The Call to Holiness and Obedience for God's People—Read "Comments" on Lev 19:1-2, 37 (242-43, 253). Leviticus 19 begins with a call to God's people to "be holy, for I the Lord your God am holy," and ends with the summation, "And you shall observe all my statutes and rules, and do them: I am the Lord." In the verses between (Lev 19:3-36), the Lord lists specific commands. Thus his people fulfill his overarching command to be holy by obeying these commands (see Section B, below). The Israelites' obedience was to be a loving and reverential response of worship to their holy King, who had called them to be a community of people who embodied his holy kingdom in the world.

1. Up to this point in Leviticus, *holiness* has referred primarily to a *ritual state* describing people, places, or objects set apart for special purposes in the Lord's tabernacle. From this point forward, holiness in Leviticus will increasingly refer to a *moral* quality. How does the commentary describe that moral quality?

2. What was the intended effect of the Israelites being set apart to embody the Lord's holiness?

3. As the scope of Leviticus 19 makes clear, holiness is not restricted to "religious" matters of personal piety but is to be pursued in all spheres of life. In other words, "*all of life* is a stage on which holiness is to be lived out" (243). List the seven spheres of life explicitly addressed in Leviticus 19 in which the Israelites were to pursue holiness:

4. The commentary describes two key purposes of obedience to the Lord's commands in Leviticus 19: an *enabling* and an *ensuring* purpose (253). Describe these purposes:

B. First Group of Commands for Holy Living—Read "Comments" on Lev 19:3-10 (243-45). Many of these verses end with the refrain "I am the Lord your God" (vv. 3, 4, 10), suggesting they form the first of three groups of commands.

1. Verse 3 commands the Israelites to honor their parents, an echo of the fifth commandment (Ex 20:12). The commentary emphasizes parents were the ones primarily responsible for their children's "covenant instruction," that is, for instructing them in the ways of the Lord and how to live in proper covenant relationship with him. Why would honoring parents be important to covenant instruction?

2. Verse 4 forbids Israelites from worshipping idols or false gods, reflecting the first and second commandments (Ex 20:3-4). Briefly describe two reasons the commentary gives for this prohibition:

3. Verses 9-10 focus on properly sharing food with those who are in need, both the poor and the resident alien or "foreigner." Briefly describe two reasons why the covenant laws for Israel often included resident aliens in the class of the disadvantaged:

C. Second Group of Commands for Holy Living: Loving Neighbors—Read "Comments" on Lev 19:11-18 (245-47). Each of these laws begins by identifying what Israelites must not do (vv. 11, 13, 15, 17) and ends with the phrase "I am the Lord" (vv. 12, 14, 16, 18), suggesting they form the second of three groups of commands. These commands to holiness pertain especially to life in community and the Lord's command to "love your neighbor as yourself" (v. 18).

1. Verses 13-14 command holiness toward hired day laborers and those with physical handicaps. What is characteristic about both of these groups, and whom do they represent (246)?

2. Verses 17-18 entail four negative commands and two positive commands concerning the ways Israelites were to respond to those who had wronged them. Briefly describe these six commands:

D. Third Group of Commands for Holy Living—Read "Comments" on Lev 19:32-36 (251-52). These laws come within a section that begins and ends by referring to keeping the Lord's statutes (vv. 19, 37), a frame that suggests vv. 19-37 form the final group of commands. Those noted below deal with loving your neighbor well.

1. Verse 32 commands the Israelites to "stand up before the gray head and honor the face of an old man" (ESV). Describe in your own words the essence of and reasons for this command:

2. Verses 33-34 and 35-36 command the Israelites to holiness by acting justly when dealing with resident aliens and more generally in legal proceedings and business transactions. Each couplet of verses provides a rationale that concerns Egypt (vv. 34, 36). Briefly describe the rationale for (a) treating foreigners justly and (b) handling legal and economic affairs honestly (252):

    a.

    b.

Read "Meaning" (253-54).

A. Imitating the Lord and His Holiness—The commands to holiness in Leviticus 19 are punctuated throughout by the phrase, "I am the Lord (your God)," which occurs no fewer than sixteen times. Thus the chapter emphasizes that the rationale for our pursuit of holiness is the sovereignty and character of the Lord himself. In this light, the commentary suggests we are called to pursue the Lord's holiness because he created us in his image to reflect that image throughout the earth (Gen 1:26-28).

1. The commentary refers to this aspect of reflecting the Lord's image as "modeling authentic humanity" to the world (253). Describe two or three practical ways in which we who follow the Lord can "model authentic humanity" to the world around us:

2. Verses 17-18 provide the Old Testament ground for the biblical admonition to "love your neighbor as yourself" (Mt 5:43; 19:19; 22:39; Mk 12:31, 33; Lk 10:27; Rom 13:9; Gal 5:14; Jas 2:8). The commentary notes that in the context of Leviticus 19, the command is to love your neighbor even when they have wronged you. We do this by addressing the wrong but always with the goal of restoring fellowship (246-47). This reflects the Lord's image in us because he himself shows generous love to those who sin against him (247). Describe two or three scenarios in which someone close to you may wrong you and how you might respond in keeping with the command of Lev 19:17-18 to "love your neighbor as yourself":

R E S P O N D

Meditate— In Leviticus 19, the Lord commands the Israelites to "be holy, for I the Lord your God am holy" (v. 2), and then gives specific commands to obey to pursue his holiness (vv. 3-36). The apostle Peter quotes from Leviticus and echoes this dynamic in the New Testament when he writes, "As obedient children, do not be conformed to the passions of your former ignorance, but as he who called you is holy, you also be holy in all your conduct, since it is written, 'You shall be holy, for I am holy'" (1 Pet 1:14-16). Peter further says the Lord's church is "being built up as a spiritual house, a holy priesthood, to offer spiritual sacrifices acceptable to God through Jesus Christ" (1 Pet

2:4-5). Meditate this week on 1 Pet 2:4-5 and what it might mean in your life to be part of this "holy priesthood" of Jesus' followers.

Take Action—In Israel, priests were called to model respect for the Lord's holiness by following his commands (holiness through obedience) and properly worshipping him. But this calling to holiness was not reserved for "official" priests alone. When the Lord called Israel, he called all the people to be his "kingdom of priests and holy nation" (Exod 19:6), that is, all were to be like priests in terms of living out God's holy values in the world and properly worshipping him. Peter picks up on this same thought for believers today when he refers to Jesus' followers as a "holy priesthood," that is, a group of people who show respect for God's holy character in the way we worship him and live out his holy values. As you meditate on 1 Pet 2:4-5 this week, be mindful of your role as part of this holy priesthood. Take a few intentional steps to live out the Lord's holiness in your own life and to worship him well. For guidance, consider the commands of Lev 19 and what it means for you to follow them today. Take a few notes on the things you tried and the results of your efforts:

THE LORD'S HOLY PRACTICES FOR HIS HOLY PEOPLE

ANALYZE

Opening Prayer

Heavenly Father, as we study your word in Leviticus, deepen our appreciation for your holiness and your passion for ours. Help us see the connection between personal holiness and our obedience to your commands. And help us to become more like you, to be holy because you are holy. We pray these things in the name of your holy Son, Jesus. Amen.

Share Reflections | 5 min.

Have each person share one reflection from the Reflect exercise on the first page of the Individual Study. You can do this in pairs, or in the larger group if you have time. This is not a time to critique or ask lots of questions of each other, but simply to share something God has put on your heart.

Clarify Issues from the Lesson | 10 min.

Back in the larger group, prepare for your discussion by clarifying any uncertainties about the Scripture or commentary, but be careful with your time. The purpose here is to focus on a few issues that may be particularly difficult, not to open a broad discussion about the lesson.

Meaning of Leviticus for Today | 20 min.

Take turns reading aloud each point below, and discuss the questions as a group.

A. An Objective Ground for Ethics—The reality that God created us in his image means we are called to reflect his character (Gen 1:26a, 27) and to respect his created order, or creational design (Gen 1:26b, 28). Leviticus 19 makes clear the basis for this calling is God's essence as pre-existent, sovereign Creator and Lord of the universe: "I am the Lord your God" (Lev 19:2). As such, God has given us an objective ground for ethics: Ethical choices are those consistent with his unchanging, perfect, holy character, and that align with his will as reflected in the design of his created order. **Discuss one or two contemporary ethical issues (for example, treatment of and provision for the needy; the widespread use of pornography; genetic engineering, such as human cloning in the pursuit of curing disease; etc.). Analyze how they might be addressed according to this objective Christian standard in contrast to other ways contemporary culture makes its ethical choices.**

B. Holiness and Immigration Policy—Leviticus 19 has a strong emphasis on holy treatment of those in Israel who were resident aliens or foreigners. Verses 9-10 command the provision of food (and by implication, other life-sustaining necessities) to foreigners sojourning in Israel to address their economic disadvantage relative to land-owning Israelites. Verses 33-34 go even further, prohibiting all wrongdoing against foreigners and commanding that they be treated as native Israelites, who are to be loved as the Israelites love themselves. **Discuss how this strong emphasis on the Lord's love for the foreigner ought to inform a Christian perspective on refugees and other immigrants in our own country. (For the purposes of this discussion, consider refugees and immigrants who have come here legally.) Analyze some specific examples of laws and policies that might reflect the Lord's holiness on this subject.**

EVALUATE

Respecting Our Elders | 20 min.

Leviticus 19 also commands us to honor and respect our elders (v. 32). This acknowledges their wisdom and the experience they have gained from many years of living and of walking with the Lord. It also shows respect for the authority of those in our community who are responsible for our guidance (251). Moreover, honoring and respecting our elders is part of extending patience and compassion to those among us who are weakening with age (252). Indeed, whether the elders be our parents (v. 3) or the seniors in our midst (v. 32), the Lord expects us to extend to them physical support and care (see 1 Tim 5:3-10, where "honoring" a widow [v. 3] includes financial care and where v. 8 commands us to care for our parents' needs). **Evaluate the treatment of elders in your own communities, including your family, church, and local civic communities. Discuss ways your communities might need to change their attitudes and practices to come in line with the Lord's call to holiness in our relationships with our elders.**

CONSEQUENCES FOR ILLICIT SEXUAL AND SPIRITUAL PRACTICES

ENGAGE

Reflect

Take time to reflect candidly on your view of sin, especially your own. How often do you think about your sin and how deeply it offends God's holiness? Why? Do you desire to view your own and others' sin as seriously as God views it? What steps might you take to align your view of sin with that of the Lord's (if you think it needs alignment)?

Pray

Heavenly Father, as I study your word in Leviticus, help me to grow in the conviction that my sin is a treasonous offense to your holiness and sovereignty. Give me the strength and willingness to lay aside my sin and pursue your holiness. Help me do this through the power of your Holy Spirit and the example of your Son Jesus, who was tempted in every way that I am, yet was without sin. I pray this in his holy name. Amen.

Read

- Read Leviticus 20, which provides the consequences for violating the commands of Leviticus 18 against illicit sexual and spiritual practices. This chapter, along with Leviticus 18 and 19, form a unit of related laws that teach Israel how to live as the Lord's holy people in contexts beyond worship at the tabernacle.
- In the commentary, read "Introduction", section 5.c (62-69), and "Context" (254).
- Read Leviticus 20 again.

UNDERSTAND

Israel was a *theocracy*, that is, a nation where God himself was King (60, 65). Leviticus 20 lays out serious consequences for conduct considered treasonous against him and his kingdom. False worship (vv. 1-5) and divination (vv. 6, 27) were direct acts of treason because they repudiated the Lord's kingship (65). Likewise, acts that undermined the family (for example, dishonoring parents, v. 9; and illicit sex, vv. 10-21) could also be considered treasonous because the family structure in Israel was so foundational and critical to the covenant relationship with the Lord (65). As the commentary notes (254), Leviticus 20 is structured as a simple chiasm: The first and last sections concern illicit spiritual practices (vv. 1-6, 27), the center section deals with illicit sexual practices (vv. 10-21), and coming in between are two exhortations for the Lord's people to be holy (vv. 7-8, 22-26). The following questions are divided according to the various components of the chiasm:[1]

A. Exhortations for the Lord's People to be Holy—Read "Comments" on Lev 20:7-8 and 22-26 (256, 259-60). In the midst of his laws concerning the consequences for illicit spiritual and sexual practices, the Lord twice exhorts his people to *live holy lives* (vv. 7-8 and 22-26):

1. Verses 7a and 8a make clear the Lord's people are to live in a holy manner by *following* the Lord's holy decrees. What is the reason vv. 7b and 8b give for that command?

2. Verses 22-24 give a second reason or motivation for living in a holy manner by following the Lord's holy decrees. Describe in your own words this reason or motivation:

3. Verse 25 interjects what at first may seem like an odd reference to ritual purity, since that is not the context of Leviticus 20. What is a likely reason the Lord mentions ritual purity at this point in Leviticus?

---

[1] Verse 9 concerns the consequences for violating the law against dishonoring parents, which is the fifth of the Ten Commandments (Ex 20:12) and is also given in Lev 19:3. Because parents were so crucial to providing covenant instruction from the Lord (see Deut 6:6-7), for an Israelite to dishonor a parent was tantamount to rejecting their covenant King. The conduct in view here is outright rebellion by adult children, not the ordinary disrespect sometimes displayed by minors. See Commentary (256-57).

B. Consequences of Illicit Spiritual Practices—Read "Comments" on Lev 20:1-5 and 27 (255-56, 260): In Leviticus 18, the Lord declares certain spiritual and sexual practices detestable and completely out of bounds for his holy people. Here in Leviticus 20, he announces the consequences for ignoring his decrees. Verses 1-5 concern the horrific practice of child sacrifice (see Lev 18:21).

1. Verse 2 announces the death penalty for anyone who sacrifices their child to the false god Molech, and makes clear that "the people of the land" (ESV), or members of the community, are to carry out the execution. Why might the community be tempted not to carry out the death penalty?

2. Verse 4 pronounces that the Lord himself will oppose those who sacrifice their children to Molech by "setting his face" against them and "cutting them off" from their people. What are two possible interpretations of this pronouncement?

3. Verse 5 reiterates the Lord's opposition but now in the context of the community failing to execute judgment against the offender. The Lord promises to set his face against and "cut off" (possibly by some sort of immediate or later death) two groups of people in the community. Briefly describe those groups:

4. Verses 6 and 27 provide for the death penalty for practices involving mediums and spiritists ("necromancers," ESV), either by the Lord himself cutting them off (v. 6) or by the community executing them (v. 27). Consult the commentary on Lev 19:31 (251) and briefly describe the nature of this illicit practice (sometimes called "divination") and why it is so offensive to the Lord:

C. Consequences of Illicit Sexual Practices—Read "Comments" on Lev 20:10-21 (257-59): As mentioned above, Leviticus 18 decrees certain sexual practices to be detestable to the Lord and unacceptable for his holy people. Here in Leviticus 20, the Lord pronounces the consequences for ignoring his decrees about illicit sex, including adultery, incest, homosexual intercourse, and bestiality.[2]

This section is divided into three parts, each providing a different consequence: the death penalty (vv. 10-16), exile from Israel (vv. 11-19), and dying childless (vv. 20-21). Leviticus does not explain why some of these sexual acts were capital offenses and others were not. What is clear, however, is that all these situations are serious, since even being "cut off" or "dying childless" were severe penalties in a society that put such high value on having an ongoing place among the covenant people of God.

1. List the seven illicit sexual practices in vv. 10-16 that were punishable by death:

2. List the three illicit sexual practices in vv. 17-19 that were punishable by being exiled ("cut off") from the nation of Israel:

3. List the two illicit sexual practices in vv. 20-21 that were punishable by dying childless, or being *deemed* childless and thus being eliminated from the genealogies of Israel:

---

[2] Verse 10 states the penalty for adultery, while vv. 11-12, 14, 17, 19-21 concern penalties for various forms of incest. The presence of the adultery law implies the incest laws did not intend to prohibit such relations only in the case of married women (otherwise, the law against adultery would have sufficed). Rather, these laws also prohibit such relations with the women while they are unmarried or their marriages have ended (through death or divorce). (For the one exception to 20:21, see comments in the commentary on 18:16, p. 234.)

Read "Meaning" (260-61).

A. The Seriousness of Sin—In many cultures today, "sin" is thought of as an outdated concept involving irrelevant religious rules. Biblically speaking, however, sin is a horrifying reality. Sin is an act of rebellion against the God who is King of our lives and an acid that damages the world of goodness, justice, mercy, and love he wants us to inhabit. Leviticus 20 deals with three areas of sin the Lord considers especially treasonous to his sovereignty and damaging to his created order: false worship or spirituality, dishonoring parents, and sex outside heterosexual marriage.

1. Briefly describe one or two examples of false worship or "spirituality" in our culture that most view as "harmless" or even acceptable and that many Christians may have accepted within the broad practice of Christianity:

2. Briefly describe one or two ways our society facilitates dishonoring parents and grandparents that Christians may have wrongly accepted as okay to do:

3. Briefly describe one or two examples of sexual practices outside heterosexual marriage that many Christians may have accepted as biblical in our modern culture:

RESPOND

Meditate—While Leviticus 20 reminds us of how seriously God takes our sin, the Lord has graciously given us his Son Jesus as an example and motivation to resist the temptation to sin and instead to pursue his holiness. Meditate this week on Heb 12:1-3: "Therefore, since we are surrounded by so great a cloud of witnesses [of Old Testament faith], let us also lay aside every weight, and sin which clings so closely, and let us run with endurance the race that is set before us, looking to Jesus, the founder and perfecter of our faith, who for the joy that was set before him endured the cross, despising the shame, and is seated at the right hand of the throne of God. Consider him who endured from sinners such hostility against himself, so that you may not grow weary or fainthearted." (ESV)

Take Action—Hebrews 12:1-3 gives us two examples as our motivation for laying aside sin: We are called to think deeply about fellow believers who have been faithful and ultimately to think about the faithfulness and endurance of Jesus. As you consider your own struggles with specific sins this week (anger, jealousy, envy, impatience, lust, and so forth), be mindful each moment of the degree to which you are trying to "lay aside" those sins. Try to write down the degree of temptation and the degree to which you are consciously laying those sins aside.

CONSEQUENCES FOR ILLICIT SEXUAL AND SPIRITUAL PRACTICES

ANALYZE

Opening Prayer

Heavenly Father, as we study your word in Leviticus, help us to grow in the conviction that our sin is a treasonous offense to your holiness and sovereignty. Give us the strength and willingness to lay aside our sin and pursue your holiness. Help us to do this through the power of your Holy Spirit and the example of your Son Jesus, who was tempted in every way we are, yet was without sin. We pray this in his holy name. Amen.

Share Reflections | 5 min.

Have each person share one reflection from the Reflect exercise on the first page of the Individual Study. You can do this in pairs, or in the larger group if you have time. This is not a time to critique or ask lots of questions of each other, but simply to share something God has put on your heart.

Clarify Issues from the Lesson | 10 min.

Back in the larger group, prepare for your discussion by clarifying any uncertainties about the Scripture or commentary, but be careful with your time. The purpose here is to focus on a few issues that may be particularly difficult, not to open a broad discussion about the lesson.

Meaning of Leviticus for Today | 20 min.

Take turns reading aloud each point below, and discuss the questions as a group.

A. Temptation To Overlook Sin in the Community—Leviticus 20:4 highlights the temptation for any community of God's people to avoid dealing with sin in their midst. In the case of Israel, where justice was carried out locally, the temptation likely related to the fact that the sinner might be a relative or friend (see comments on 19:15-16, p. 246). The same temptation exists in the church today, but the strong counsel of the New Testament exhorts us to resist such temptation. For example, Paul in 1 Cor 5:1-10 rebukes the Corinthian church for allowing sexual immorality in their community to go undisciplined, a rebuke that would apply more broadly to situations where sin is not taken seriously in a church.

1. To what degree to you feel your community or fellowship is inclined to follow the negative example of the Corinthian church? Why do you feel this way?

2. Identify one or two specific sins you think probably persist in many Christian communities because those communities have not addressed them as Scripture commands. Discuss why you think this is the case.

B. Pop Spirituality in the Church—Leviticus 20:6 and 27 explicitly forbid the practice of "divination" or spiritism; that is, of seeking spiritual guidance from any source other than the Lord. This is especially abhorrent to God because it indicates we do not trust him with our lives and futures. Palm reading, fortune telling, and astrology are classic examples of modern spiritism. In addition, more versions of "new age" spirituality multiply each year through popular television programs, books and other media. Yet at least some Christians seem to consider them harmless, or even supplemental to Christian spirituality. **Discuss this phenomenon and why you think these practices are accepted by some Christians.**

EVALUATE

The New Christian Sexual Ethic | 20 min.

Both the Old and New testaments make clear that the Lord's people are not to engage in sex outside heterosexual marriage (Gen 2:24; Ex 20:10-21; Lev 18:6-18, 22; 20:10-17, 19-21; Deut 22:28-29; Mt 5:27-28; 1 Cor 7:2, 8-9; 1 Thess 4:3-5). Yet it's also clear that a significant number of confessing Christians in the West do not follow this ethic. **Discuss what you have observed about this dynamic in your community and among your Christian friends and acquaintances, and evaluate why you think this dynamic persists:**

COMMANDS FOR PRIESTS TO REVERE THE LORD'S HOLY THINGS

ENGAGE

Reflect

We rightly think of the Lord as holy, but how often do you ponder the holiness of his possessions? Indeed, how often do you think of the Lord as possessing things? Take time to reflect on this. What does the Lord possess? What doesn't he possess? Which of his possessions should we consider to be sacred or holy? Reflect on how you treat the Lord's holy possessions and how you honor them as holy or sacred.

Pray

Heavenly Father, as I study your word in Leviticus, help me grow in my appreciation for the passion you have for your holy possessions, especially for your church, a holy nation and a people for your own possession that you have claimed for yourself through the precious blood of your Son, Jesus, in whose holy name I pray. Amen.

Read

- Read Leviticus 21, which begins a new section of laws in Lev 21-24 concerning the due reverence the priests and people of Israel owed to the Lord's holy things and holy times.
- In the commentary, read the preface and "Context" paragraphs (262-63).
- Read Leviticus 21 again.

UNDERSTAND

A. Commands for Priests and the High Priest to Revere the Lord's Holy Things—Read "Comments" on Lev 21-22:16 (263) and 21:1-15 (263-67). Leviticus 21 concerns the standard of care the Lord required of Israel's priests toward his holy possessions, including the priests themselves.

1. This section of Leviticus teaches that the priests were held to a higher standard than other Israelites. Briefly summarize the two main reasons for this higher standard:

2. Mourning for the dead typically resulted in ritual impurity (likely because of close contact with the ritually defiling corpse). Since priests were ritually holy, they were normally not allowed to become ritually defiled in this way. However, the Lord graciously allowed an exception for priests in certain cases of mourning (vv. 2-3). Briefly describe the <u>nature</u> and <u>extent</u> of that exception:

3. Lev 21:4 does <u>not</u> provide the same mourning exception for deceased relatives related to the priest by marriage. The commentary suggests a priest's wife would nonetheless be included in the exception. Briefly describe the argument for this:

4. Lev 21:7-8 also concern the holiness of the priests as the Lord's possession in the context of their marriages. Read the "Additional Note" at the end of this lesson for a fuller (and revised) explanation of 21:7. Summarize the reasons given there for the prohibitions of this verse.

5. Adult sons or daughters who showed great disrespect to their parents were guilty of a capital crime (see at 20:9, 256-57). Leviticus 21:9 deals with the crime of a priest's daughter engaging as a prostitute. Describe briefly why this crime was doubly severe and why the sin against her father was also a sin against the Lord:

6. Verses 10-15 concern mourning and marriage commands specific to the high priest, whom the Lord held to an even higher standard than other priests. What was one significant way the <u>mourning</u> commands were more restrictive for the high priest?

7. Verses 13-15 command that the high priest marry only a virgin and only from his tribe of Levi. What two important effects does the commentary suggest were achieved by these requirements?

B. Descendants of Aaron Who Could Not Minister as Priests: Read "Comments" on Lev 21:16-23 (267-69). Israel's priests were to come from the tribe of Levi and be descendants of Aaron. While the first part of Leviticus 21 focuses on them maintaining their holy status so they can serve the Lord in his tabernacle, the second half concerns certain physical "blemishes" (ESV) or "defects" (NIV) that would prevent them from serving because the defects would profane or defile the Lord's holy precincts—places in the tabernacle used for worship, such as the altar and the Most Holy Place behind the tabernacle curtain (269).

1. Leviticus does not explain why physical defects would profane the Lord's precincts. But the commentary suggests two possible explanations relating to symbolism. Briefly describe in your own words these two possible explanations:

2. The laws of Leviticus allocated the Lord's food offerings between holy and most holy offerings. The priest's families could partake of the holy offerings, but only the priests themselves could eat the most holy offerings. What about Lev 21:22 shows that Aaron's descendants with physical defects were still considered priests to the Lord, even though they were not permitted to minister in his holy precincts?

APPLY

Read "Meaning" (269-70)

A. Disrespecting the Lord's Holy Possessions—In 1 Cor 6:12-20 the apostle Paul says "we are not our own" because we have been "bought with a price," referring to the costliness of Jesus' death on our behalf. In other words, those who are in Christ now belong to the Lord as his holy possessions (Tit 2:14; 1 Pet 2:9). One of the overarching themes of Leviticus 21 is that disrespecting the Lord's holy possessions is tantamount to disrespecting the Lord himself (262). **Write a brief reflection on the how 1 Cor 6:12-20 is an application of Leviticus 21:**

B. Priests Held to a Higher Standard—An overarching theme of Leviticus 21 is that the Lord held priests to a higher standard of holiness than lay Israelites. The New Testament carries forward this same principle (Jas 3:1). **If you are a leader in your church, how should this principle of Leviticus 21 affect how you conduct yourself in ministry? If you are not a church leader, how should this same principle affect how you interact with and pray for your leaders (compare Lev 21:8; Heb 13:17)?**

RESPOND

Meditate: Leviticus 21 prohibited Aaron's descendants from ministering as priests if they had certain physical defects or "blemishes." While Scripture gives no rationale for this prohibition, it seems clear that it was symbolic, relating to the holiness of the office of priest (267-69). Indeed, when viewed in light of the New Testament, we see that the Lord's requirement of unblemished or "perfect" priests foreshadowed the perfect priesthood of Jesus. Meditate this week on Heb 7:26-28: "For it was indeed fitting that we should have such a high priest, holy, innocent, unstained, separated from sinners, and exalted above the heavens. He has no need, like those high priests, to offer sacrifices daily, first for his own sins and then for those of the people, since he did this once for all when he offered up himself. For the law appoints men in their weakness as high priests, but the word of the oath, which came later than the law, appoints a Son who has been made perfect forever" (ESV).

Take Action: As the commentary notes (268-69), the fact that Aaron's descendants who had physical "blemishes" were welcome with other priests to eat the most holy food offerings at "the King's table" underscores the Lord's honor and love for people with physical impairments (v. 22; cf. 2 Sam 9; Lk 14:21). As you go about your week, try to be aware of your interactions with people who have physical disabilities, asking yourself whether you treat them in such a way that, if places were reversed, would make you feel like a welcome, loved and honored guest.

COMMANDS FOR PRIESTS TO REVERE THE LORD'S HOLY THINGS

ANALYZE

Opening Prayer

Heavenly Father, as we study your word in Leviticus, help us grow in our appreciation for the passion you have for your holy possessions, especially for your church, a holy nation and a people for your own possession that you have claimed for yourself through the precious blood of your Son, Jesus, in whose holy name we pray. Amen.

Share Reflections | 5 min.

Have each person share one reflection from the Reflect exercise on the first page of the Individual Study. You can do this in pairs, or in the larger group if you have time. This is not a time to critique or ask lots of questions of each other, but simply to share something God has put on your heart.

Clarify Issues from the Lesson | 10 min.

Back in the larger group, prepare for your discussion by clarifying any uncertainties about the Scripture or commentary, but be careful with your time. The purpose here is to focus on a few issues that may be particularly difficult, not to open a broad discussion about the lesson.

Meaning of Leviticus for Today | 20 min.

Take turns reading aloud each point below, and discuss the questions as a group:

A. High Standard of Holiness for the Shepherds of God's People—Leviticus 21 demonstrates that the Lord holds those who lead his people to a higher standard of holiness (cf. 1 Tim 3:1-3; Heb 13:17; Jas 3:1). The commentary suggests at least two possible reasons for this: First, by living to a higher standard of holiness, the Lord's leaders are able to continue ministering in their special roles, and second, they are able to communicate properly to others the values of the Lord (263).

  1. Discuss why living to a higher standard of holiness enables the leaders of God's church to continue ministering in their special roles, and analyze several hypothetical situations where this would clearly be demonstrated.

2.   Discuss why living to a higher standard of holiness enables the leaders of God's church to communicate properly to others the values of the Lord, and analyze several hypothetical situations where this would clearly be demonstrated.

B. Leaving the Sanctuary to Mourn—Lev 21:12 prohibited the high priest from leaving his duties in the sanctuary to participate in ritually defiling mourning practices, such as altering his appearance or being near a corpse, which would have prevented him from ministering before the Lord (266). Obviously, this was a hardship for the high priest, since mourning our dead is an important ritual for personal and community life. Thankfully, Jesus' high priesthood has done away with the Old Testament office of high priest (Heb 9:11-12) so that such mourning restrictions no longer apply to God's ministers, who are now free to "mourn with those who mourn" (Rom 12:15, NIV). **Evaluate the relative importance of a church leader mourning with congregation members, and discuss specific ways church leaders should be encouraged to mourn with others.**

EVALUATE

Helping Our Leaders Live Holy Lives | 20 min.

Lev 21:8 commanded the Israelites to regard the priest as holy and to "sanctify him" (ESV), or "make sure he is holy" (Hartley, 1992: 342). In the context of Leviticus 21, this meant helping the priest maintain his ritually holy status (265). Discuss several ways a church congregation might help their pastors, elders, and other leaders live holy lives before the Lord.

ADDITIONAL NOTE ON LEV 21:7-8

(Jay now prefers to explain Lev 21:7-8 in a different way. The following note is slightly adapted from a second, longer commentary on Leviticus that he is writing for Zondervan.)[1]

Commands about marriage (21:7–8)—"A woman profaned by prostitution they must not marry, and a woman divorced from her husband they must not marry, for holy is [a priest] to his God" (21:7; my translation). This law is not answering the question, "Can these women (re)marry?"[2] It is answering the question, "Can a priest marry them?" The answer is, "No, because of the priest's holiness." But how does the priest's holiness connect to the prohibition against marrying the women named here? We may consider the cases one at a time.

"A woman profaned by prostitution" is more woodenly translated "a woman, a prostitute and profaned." This suggests that the verse is not describing a former way of life (she was a prostitute and profaned herself) but a current one (she is a prostitute and is profaned). Such sexual immorality was to be avoided by all of the LORD's holy people, but especially by the priests, who were to set a model of holy life and behavior and to be at the complete opposite end of the spectrum when it comes to sin and defilement. Indeed, such a prohibition may have been especially important at this point in Israel's history because the risks of such behavior in connection with a holy place were incredibly high. In the ancient Near East, prostitution could be connected with temples, a connection forbidden to the Israelites (Deut 23:17 – 18). This prohibition would have prevented priests from being involved in such activity.

Identifying the rationale behind the prohibition against marrying a divorcée is more tentative because the Bible does not provide a lot of information about divorce in ancient Israel. It is possible, however, that this prohibition is also connected to sexual immorality. This is not because divorce is always due to sexual immorality, but because it can be, in at least two different ways. First, and simply, sexual immorality was one of the reasons for divorce. If the divorce was due to the wife's unfaithfulness, this law would again keep holy priests separate from the sin and its defilement. Second, there was also a potential for sexual immorality this law would have prevented, namely, a situation in which a wife asks for a divorce, not for any valid biblical reason, but because she and the priest had fallen in love. Such a divorce would be a technical way to avoid the charge of adultery—she was no longer married to her husband and so could marry and have relations with the priest—but it was really a way of using divorce in order to have an affair. This law made it impossible for such a situation to be viewed legitimately.[3]

---

[1] Jay Sklar, *Leviticus: A Discourse Analysis of the Hebrew Bible* (Grand Rapids, MI: Zondervan, forthcoming).

[2] The fact that priests alone are forbidden from marrying them suggests (re)marriage did at times happen for these women. With regard to divorce in particular, the Old Testament presumes that it can be legitimate, especially for sexual immorality. It would be natural to imply that remarriage of the wronged party was allowable at least in these circumstances.

[3] It is natural to ask, "What about a situation where the divorce was not the woman's fault? Or where she had justification for divorcing her husband?" These exceptions are not named, perhaps because if they were, the priests may have abused their power to make use of them, and preyed on women by convincing them to divorce their husbands in order to marry them. The hard and fast nature of this

While the above explanations must remain tentative, it may be said with more confidence that other texts make clear the Lord's commands in general are not meant to isolate the divorcée, e.g., a priest's daughter who is divorced is not an outcast, but can be freely welcomed back to her father's home—and even to eat of the holy food put aside for the priest's family (22:13). In 21:7, the Lord's commands are also not meant to isolate the divorcée; rather, they are meant to help priests to continue in holiness. This was not only for the leaders' good, but for the good of the people as a whole, who needed holy priests to lead them in the ways of the LORD and to minister on their behalf before him.

It may finally be noted that in its description of qualifications for spiritual leaders in the church, the New Testament continues to emphasize the importance of spiritual leaders being holy in their conduct and above reproach; it does not, however, repeat the prohibitions of this particular verse (1 Tim 3:1–13; 4:12; Titus 1:5–10). It was undoubtedly assumed that church leaders could not marry someone currently working as a prostitute, but what about a former prostitute or a divorcée? It could be that these were also assumed to be out of bounds, so much so that they did not need to be mentioned. But it seems more likely to me they are not mentioned because the sacrifice of Jesus so thoroughly cleanses all sin, and thus the defilement of the repentant believer so deeply, that women in these situations are now to be viewed as holy if they have given their lives to Jesus, and thus able to marry even leaders in the church.

---

law would have protected against such abuse. To come at this from a complementary angle: exceptions are perhaps not named because of the important role of the priest for society. To this day, certain jobs have extra strict requirements (e.g., air traffic control operators, nuclear plant operators, train conductors). Activities that are allowed for other jobs (e.g., having a drink before starting a shift) are not allowed for these jobs, and there are no exceptions. This is because so many people's lives depend on that person doing their job properly; the extra strict requirements are meant to prevent certain activities from happening that could compromise the person's work, not simply for the sake of the person in the job, but for all those whose lives depend on them. The same is no less true here: the Israelites' very lives depended on priests leading them properly in the Lord's holy ways and in interceding on their behalf before him. Therefore, the priests have extra strict requirements that are meant to prevent certain activities from happening that could compromise their work (and thus put the people in jeopardy as well).

LEVITICUS 22

COMMANDS FOR PRIESTS AND PEOPLE TO REVERE THE LORD'S HOLY SACRIFICES

ENGAGE

Reflect

Take time to reflect on your attitudes and behaviors concerning worship of the Lord. How do you define worship in terms of your vocation, talents, and free time? To what extent do you consider your worship of the Lord as a holy or sacred activity? Why? Should you be treating worship with more reference as a sacred endeavor? If so, how might you alter your attitudes or behaviors?

Pray

Heavenly Father, as I study your word in Leviticus, deepen my sense of the sacredness of your holy church, of your presence among those whom you have redeemed, of the ministry of your saints, and of our proper worship of you as our redeeming God. I pray this in the holy name of your Son, Jesus. Amen.

Read

- Read Leviticus 22, which is part of the section of laws in Lev 21-24 concerning reverence the priests and other people of Israel owed to the Lord's holy things and holy times.
- In the commentary, review the preface and "Context" paragraphs (262-63).
- Read Leviticus 22 again.

A. Commands to Priests for Treating the Lord's Sacred Offerings Properly—Read "Comments" and "Meaning" on Lev 22:1-9 (270-71). The summary command of Lev 22:2 warns Aaron and his descendants, the priests, to "treat with respect" (NIV) various food offerings the people offered to the Lord, which were thus sacred.

1. Identify the five types of sacred food offerings mentioned in the commentary (270):

2. Why would it show great disrespect for a priest to "come near" (NIV) or "approach" (ESV) the sacred offerings while he was ritually impure?

3. In verse 9, the Lord declares that he is the one who "sanctifies" (ESV) or "makes holy" (NIV) the priests. What definition does the commentary give for the Lord "making holy" or "sanctifying" someone?

B. Commands to Priests for Guarding the Sacred Offerings—Read "Comments" and "Meaning" on Lev 22:10-16 (271-73). The Lord called the priests not only to handle his sacred offerings properly but also to guard them from mishandling by lay Israelites.

1. The Lord had given the sacred offerings to the priests and their households for food, and no one outside their households could eat them. What three categories of people mentioned in verses 10 and 12 could not eat of the sacred offerings?

2. Verses 11 and 13 clarify two categories of people the Lord considered to be part of the priest's household and who could therefore eat the sacred offerings. Briefly describe these two categories:

3. Verses 15 and 16 summarize the priests' responsibility for guarding the sacred offerings from lay Israelites. What would be the result if the priests failed?

C. Commands to Priests and Lay People to Respect the Lord's Holy Sacrifices—Read "Comments" on Lev 22:17-30 and "Meaning" (273-76). This section focuses on the Lord's acceptance of sacrificial offerings; that is, his responding with favor and pleasure to an offering and therefore to the offeror. This section is addressed to both the priests and lay Israelites.

1. Two things were required for an offering to be accepted by the Lord. The first is addressed in vv. 17-25 and the second in vv. 26-30. What were they?

2. Verses 22-24 list twelve physical defects or "blemishes" (ESV) that would disqualify a sacrificial animal as a proper burnt offering for freewill and vow offerings. This list parallels in several ways the list of twelve blemishes in Leviticus 21 that disqualified a priest from ministering in the Lord's sanctuaries. At the very least, what do such parallels underscore?

3. Verses 29-30 concern the proper time for eating a thank offering to the Lord so that it would be accepted. Briefly describe the timing for eating such an offering:

D. Concluding Commands to Obedience—Read "Comment" on Lev 22:31-33 (276). Like many of the preceding chapters in Leviticus, this one concludes with strong commands to obey its laws. Two biblical themes combine here to provide the Israelites with a reason for obedience: First, the Lord is their Redeemer who brought them out of Egypt to be their God. Second, as their redeeming God, he is above all, holy.

1. What was it about the Lord as their Redeemer that called the Israelites to obey him as an act of grateful worship?

2. Why did the Lord's holiness require that the Israelites obey him?

3. The commentary notes that the Lord does not simply rescue his people from slavery. What else does he do in this context?

APPLY

A. Set Apart by the Lord to Live Holy Lives—In Lev 22:9, the Lord declares he is the one who sanctifies the priests. This means he has set apart the priests to live in a holy manner (271). The New Testament likewise declares that those who are united with Christ have been called by the Lord as a royal priesthood (1 Pet 2:5, 9). **Write a brief reflection on what you think it might mean to be "set apart" in your cultural context to live in a holy manner as one of the Lord's royal priests.**

B. Guarding the Holiness of Others—Leviticus 22:10-16 placed a special responsibility on the priests to guard the Lord's sacred food offerings so lay Israelites did not eat them and thus profane his holy possessions and name. The New Testament shows a similar concern that each of us guard our brothers and sisters in the Lord to help them pursue holy lives (cf. Gal 6:1-3; Col 3:16; 1 Thess 5:14; Heb 3:13; 12:15-16; Jas 5:19-20). **What are two or three areas in the lives of your brothers or sisters in Christ where you think you should be diligent to guard their holiness, and what are some ways you might pursue this responsibility?**

RESPOND

Meditate—In Lev 22:32 the Lord declares, "I am the Lord who sanctifies you." Meditate this week on Jesus' high priestly prayer in John 17:17-19, where he asks our heavenly Father to sanctify each of us in the truth: "Sanctify them in the truth; your word is truth. As you sent me into the world, so I have sent them into the world. And for their sake I consecrate myself, that they also may be sanctified in truth." (ESV)

Take Action—Leviticus 22 closes with the Lord's reminder to the people of Israel that he is the Lord who sanctifies them and brought them out of slavery from the land of Egypt to be their God. As you consider this week what it means to be "set apart" by the Lord to live a holy life, take time to reflect on and note the aspects of your life that the Lord has redeemed and is still redeeming and to thank him for his redemption in these areas.

COMMANDS FOR PRIESTS AND PEOPLE TO REVERE THE LORD'S HOLY SACRIFICES

ANALYZE

Opening Prayer

Heavenly Father, as we study your word in Leviticus, deepen our sense of the sacredness of your holy church, of your presence among those whom you have redeemed, of the ministry of your saints, and of our proper worship of you as our redeeming God. We pray this in the holy name of your Son, Jesus. Amen.

Share Reflections | 5 min.

Have each person share one reflection from the Reflect exercise on the first page of the Individual Study. You can do this in pairs, or in the larger group if you have time. This is not a time to critique or ask lots of questions of each other, but simply to share something God has put on your heart.

Clarify Issues from the Lesson | 10 min.

Back in the larger group, prepare for your discussion by clarifying any uncertainties about the Scripture or commentary, but be careful with your time. The purpose here is to focus on a few issues that may be particularly difficult, not to open a broad discussion about the lesson.

Meaning of Leviticus for Today | 20 min.

Take turns reading aloud each point below, and discuss the questions as a group:

A. Respecting the Lord's Holiness Through Proper Worship—Leviticus 22:17-30 basically concerns honoring God's holiness by offering him proper worship. For the Israelites, proper worship included offering proper sacrificial animals and following proper sacrificial procedures (273). Under the new covenant in Jesus' blood, we are no longer under the Old Testament sacrificial system. Nevertheless, the New Testament makes clear that we are to continue worshiping the Lord in proper ways (see Acts 2:42; Rom 12:1; 1 Cor 11:17-34; 14:1-40; Eph 4:1-6; 5:18-21; Col 3:15-17; Heb 10:23-25; 12:28-29; Rev 1:10). **Without debating worship styles, music preferences, or other areas of Christian liberty, discuss some aspects of proper worship that all believers should be able to affirm; likewise, discuss behaviors or activities that should be considered inappropriate worship of the Lord.**

B. Moral Purity Among Spiritual Leaders—Leviticus 22:3 prohibited any priest who was ritually impure from "coming near" the altar to offer sacrifices so as not to disrespect or profane the Lord's holy name. Likewise, the New Testament continues this concern in the realm of moral purity, requiring church members who fall into sin to be disciplined, including being removed from spiritual leadership, even if only for a time (cf. Mt 18:15-17; Rom 16:17; 1 Cor 5:2, 11; 2 Cor 13:1-3; Eph 5:3; 1 Tim 5:19-20; Tit 3:10-11; Heb 12:15-16). Sexual immorality is an obvious case for disciplining and removing a church member from a leadership role. **Discuss other forms of immorality that ought to raise serious questions about whether a member should be involved in spiritual leadership and what forms of discipline and restoration should be followed in such cases:**

EVALUATE

Treating the Sacred Things of God with Reverence | 20 min.

As we have seen, the overall theme of Leviticus 21 and 22 can be summarized as the Lord's command that his people treat his sacred possessions with great reverence. In the context of both Leviticus and the New Testament, the Lord's holy possessions are especially his people, his church, and his worship. **Discuss three or four concrete ways your church or small group might excel in treating the Lord's sacred possessions with reverence.**

Observing the Lord's Holy Times

ENGAGE

Reflect

Think about your typical week: How often do you remember the Lord, his character, his actions on your behalf, and his relationship with you as your Redeemer? Why do you think this is? Reflect on your obedience and disobedience to the Lord: What is the relationship between your obedience and "remembering" the Lord? Why? What are some practical steps you might take during your week to remember the Lord more consistently and reverently?

Pray

Heavenly Father, as I study your word in Leviticus, help me to remember your character, your actions on my behalf, and your relationship with me as my Redeemer. Grow in me a passion for celebrating your power and grace in my life and for observing your Sabbath each week as a way of remembering your goodness to me. I pray in the name of your Son, Jesus. Amen.

Read

- Read Leviticus 23, which is part of the section of laws in Lev 21-24 concerning reverence the priests and other people of Israel owed to the Lord's holy things and holy times.
- In the commentary, read "Context" (276-77) and review the chart of holy times (278-79).
- Read Leviticus 23 again.

UNDERSTAND

A. Introduction, and Weekly Holy Time of Sabbath—Read "Comments" on Lev 23:1-3 (277, 280).

1. What are the two themes introduced by verse 2?

2. The Israelites were to celebrate the appointed times of Leviticus 23 as "holy gatherings" (Sklar), setting them apart as holy to the Lord. What two things did this entail?

3. The Sabbath was a sign of the Israelites' covenant relationship with the Lord. What two things did they accomplish by observing the Sabbath?

B. Annual Holy Times in the First Half of the Year—Read "Comments" on Lev 23:4-22 (280-84). Verse 4 reintroduces the two themes of Leviticus 23 in connection with annual holy times: the "appointed times" of the Lord are Israel's religious holidays, and they are to be "holy gatherings" set apart by Israel as holy to the Lord.

1. What was the purpose in the Israelites celebrating the Passover (Lev 23:5)?

2. What did the Israelites accomplish by celebrating the Passover in the first month of the year?

3. Why is the Passover a fitting metaphor for explaining the death of Jesus?

4. What did the Israelites remember by eating only unleavened bread during the Festival of Unleavened Bread (Lev 23:6-8)?

5. Why does the commentary suggest the timing of Jesus' death and resurrection during the Festival of Unleavened Bread is fitting?

6. During the offering of firstfruits (Lev 23:9-14), the Israelites were to bring a sheaf of the first grain of their harvest as an offering to the Lord. What did this <u>acknowledge</u> and <u>declare</u>?

7. The Festival of Weeks (Lev 23:15-22) was known by various names, including Pentecost, after the Greek word for "fiftieth" (*pentekostos*), since it occurred on the fiftieth day after the offering of firstfruits. What did this festival celebrate?

8. The offering of firstfruits and Festival of Weeks celebrated the Lord's provision in the new land of Canaan, where he was leading his people Israel. What purpose did these celebrations serve with regard to the Canaanite gods worshipped in Canaan?

C. Annual Holy Times in the Second Half of the Year—Read "Comments" on Lev 23:23-43 (284-86). The holy times described in this last section all took place during the seventh month, making that month particularly significant and perhaps serving as another reminder of the Sabbath and the covenant it signified.

1. The day of trumpet blasts (Lev 23:23-25) was a "reminder proclaimed with trumpet blasts" (Sklar). What two things were signified by the Lord remembering someone?

2. What did it signify in other Old Testament contexts for a trumpet to be sounded?

3. Leviticus 23:26-32 describes the Day of Atonement, known today as Yom Kippur. What was the significance of: (a) observing the Day of Atonement, and (b) failing to observe it?

4. Leviticus 23:33-43 describes the Feast of Booths. When the Lord delivered the Israelites from Egypt, not everyone had tents, so they had to construct temporary shelters ("booths") made from branches. What were the Israelites to teach their descendants and remind themselves about the Lord as they dwelled in booths during this festival?

D. **Conclusion**—Read "Comment" on Lev 23:44 and "Meaning" (286-87).

1. What did the Lord's institution of the appointed times of Leviticus 23 (a) help the Israelites remember, and (b) enable them to do?

2. How are these purposes reflected in the Lord's Supper?

APPLY

A. Celebrating the Lord in our Gatherings—One of the enduring values Leviticus 23 carries forward for Christians today is the need for the Lord's people to remember together his character (who he is), how he has acted on our behalf in the world, and what it means to be in covenant relationship with him. This is particularly reflected in our gathering together at the Lord's Supper, which Jesus himself instituted as a remembrance of his love, his sacrifice, and his unity with those who have received forgiveness through his blood (Lk 22:14-19; Mt 26:26-29). The Christian Church has also traditionally celebrated other holidays, such as Christmas, Good Friday, and Easter, that have the potential for remembering the Lord's character, actions, and relationship with us. **Take a few moments and write down specific, creative ways you and your family or friends might celebrate these or other holidays to purposefully remember the Lord in ways described above:**

RESPOND

Meditate—The "appointed times" of Leviticus 23 were meant to help the Israelites remember the Lord's faithfulness, power, and grace on their behalf (286-87). When they forgot these things, they were quick to doubt his care for them (Ex 15:24; 16:2-3; 17:1-3) and to disobey (Ex 32:1-6; cf. Deut 8:11-14). Indeed, it is almost Moses' theme in Deuteronomy as he gives his final sermon to the children of Israel, admonishing them time and again to "remember" the Lord and what he had done for them and how they had responded (Deut 5:15; 7:18; 8:2, 18; 9:7, 27; 15:15; 16:3, 12; 24:9, 18, 22; 25:17; 32:7). This week, meditate on Ps 105:4-6: "Seek the Lord and his strength; seek his presence continually! Remember the wondrous works he has done, his miracles, and the judgments he uttered, O offspring of Abraham, his servant, children of Jacob, his chosen ones!" (ESV)

Take Action—In the Old Testament, a connection is made between "forgetting" the Lord and turning to idolatry (cf. Deut 8:19). Paul makes it clear that we are not immune from this temptation today (cf. 1 Cor 10:1-14). Take time this week to reflect on how you may be tempted to turn from the Lord to idols, and spend some time in prayer remembering the Lord's provision and blessings in your life, and thanking him for those things.

OBSERVING THE LORD'S HOLY TIMES

--- ANALYZE ---

Opening Prayer

Heavenly Father, as we study your word in Leviticus, help us to remember your character, your actions on our behalf, and your relationship with us as our Redeemer. Grow in us a passion for celebrating your power and grace in our lives, and for observing your Sabbath each week as a way of remembering your goodness to us. We pray in the name of your Son, Jesus. Amen.

Share Reflections | 5 min.

Have each person share one reflection from the Reflect exercise on the first page of the Individual Study. You can do this in pairs, or in the larger group if you have time. This is not a time to critique or ask lots of questions of each other, but simply to share something God has put on your heart.

Clarify Issues from the Lesson | 10 min.

Back in the larger group, prepare for your discussion by clarifying any uncertainties about the Scripture or commentary, but be careful with your time. The purpose here is to focus on a few issues that may be particularly difficult, not to open a broad discussion about the lesson.

Meaning of Leviticus for Today | 20 min.

Take turns reading aloud each point below, and discuss the questions as a group:

A. Helping Your Community Remember the Lord—As we noted in the Individual Study, one of the enduring values that Leviticus 23 carries forward for Christians today is the need for the Lord's people to remember together his character (who he is), how he has acted on our behalf in the world, and what it means to be in covenant relationship with him. This value is particularly reflected in the Lord's Supper, which Jesus himself instituted as a remembrance of his love, his sacrifice, and his unity with those who have received forgiveness through his blood (Lk 22:14-19; Mt 26:26-29). But opportunities abound for Christian communities to gather and remember the Lord in this way, including during weekly worship services. **Discuss some ways your church or small group might be more intentional about structuring its gatherings, celebrations, and corporate worship to better remember the Lord's character, actions, and relationship with us:**

B. The Lord's Supper as a "Holy Gathering"—The appointed times and festivals of Leviticus 23 were intended as "holy gatherings" (Sklar) that the Israelites were called to set aside as holy to the Lord, ceasing from their work and engaging in the specified rituals of remembrance (277). These holy gatherings are always intended to be community celebrations, where brothers and sisters come together to strengthen and encourage one another to live holy lives before the Lord. As noted above, the Lord's Supper is the primary New Testament gathering for this purpose (281). **Analyze your own church's practices in celebrating the Lord's Supper in terms of its nature as a robust community ritual: Are you confessing and repenting of sins to one another in community? Are you experiencing relational healing in community, either leading up to the Lord's Supper, during it, or in response it? If not, what might be done differently? Are brothers and sisters connecting and reconnecting as a result of this time? What are some others ways in which you might celebrate the Lord's Supper as a "holy gathering" unto the Lord?**

CREATE

Encouraging Sabbath Remembrance of the Lord | 20 min.

Leviticus 23 reinforces the Sabbath as a weekly holy time before the Lord, calling us to rest from our work and reaffirm our covenant relationship with the Lord, acknowledging him as the creator of all things (277), including all the blessings and provision we experience. Many Christians today apparently view the Sabbath as optional or no longer applicable in the New Testament age. But the Sabbath is rooted in creation and thus equally applicable today as it was for ancient Israel (Ex 20:11). **Discuss some practical steps your small group or church might take to instruct, encourage, and creatively motivate your fellow brothers and sisters to observe a weekly Sabbath to the Lord:**

LEVITICUS 24

CONTINUAL RITES IN THE HOLY PLACE, AND REVERING THE LORD'S HOLY NAME

ANALYZE

Reflect

How would you describe your awareness of the Lord's presence with you in your everyday life? Why do you think that's the case? What events or situations in your life tend to increase your awareness of his presence? What events or situations tend to minimize it? What are some steps you might take to become more continually aware of the Lord's constant presence with you?

Pray

Heavenly Father, as I study your word in Leviticus, help me to become more continually aware of your presence with me at all times and your indwelling presence in my heart through your Holy Spirit. Strengthen my will to continually serve you by surrendering my life to your Son, my Lord Jesus, in whose name I pray. Amen.

Read

- Read Leviticus 24, which is part of the section of laws in Lev 21-24 concerning reverence the priests and other people of Israel owed to the Lord's holy things and holy times.
- In the commentary, read "Context" (287 and 290).
- Read Leviticus 24 again.

A. Continual Rites in the Lord's Holy Place—Read "Comments" on Lev 24:1-9 and "Meaning" (288-90). Leviticus 23 described several holy festivals, including the festivals of Weeks (23:15-22) and Booths (23:33-26, 39-43). During these festivals, the men of Israel brought offerings of harvest produce to the tabernacle. Chapter 24 follows naturally, with verses 1-9 describing how some of that produce was used in two holy rites of the tabernacle: *lighting the lamps* (which used olive oil, vv. 1-4) and *placing the bread of the presence* (which used fine flour, vv. 5-9).

1. For lighting the lamps in the Holy Place of the tabernacle, only "pure oil from beaten olives" (ESV) was to be used. This was more expensive than pressed olive oil. What is one implication of requiring this more expensive oil?

2. The priests were to keep the lamps burning continually through the night (v. 3). The light represented the Lord's presence within the tabernacle. Identify the two purposes mentioned in the commentary for the priests keeping the lamps burning continually:

3. Why was the bread that the priests placed on the gold table called the bread of the Presence?

4. The Lord referred to the frankincense placed with the bread of the Presence as a "memorial portion," v. 7 (ESV). What was the meaning of that title?

5. Verse 8 refers to the bread of the Presence as a "lasting covenant" or "covenant forever" (ESV). The priests were to eat the bread in a holy place as a "most holy portion out of the Lord's food offering" (ESV) on behalf of all the tribes of Israel (cf. Ex 24:9-11). What did the priests confirm when they ate the bread of the Presence?

6. The "Meaning" discussion (289-90) identifies four actions specified in Lev 24:1-9 and four symbolic meanings of those actions. Briefly describe the four actions and meanings:

B. Revering the Lord's Holy Name—Read "Comments" on Lev 24:10-23 and "Meaning" (290-95). This section contains a special warning to all within Israel—whether native Israelite or resident alien—to honor the Lord by revering his holy name. In the narrative portion of this section, Moses inquires of the Lord about the proper application of the law against blasphemy as applied to a resident alien (vv. 10-12).

1. The man involved in this situation had an Egyptian father, so he was apparently considered a resident alien, not a native Israelite. He cursed the name of the Lord (v. 11).[1] From the example in 2 Samuel 16, what three elements are involved in cursing a superior?

2. As applied to Leviticus 24, the above means the offender had not used the Lord's name as a swear word, but had done something much worse. What had he done, and what did that demonstrate about his view of the Lord?

3. The Lord announced his verdict, which began with the order to take the blasphemer outside the camp. What is the likely reason executions took place outside the camp?

---

[1] A better translation of verse 11 is, "and the Israelite woman's son spoke the Name and cursed it."

4. The punishment in this case was death by stoning. In ancient Israel, as in many cultures, treason was a capital crime, since it is both a personal offense against the king and a danger to the well-being of the kingdom and its people. Why is it not surprising that cursing a king would be considered a capital offense like treason?

5. Verses 15-22 set forth several principles of justice. These may have been placed in the middle of the narrative as further elaboration about how justice should be applied, since Moses had just made such an inquiry. Briefly describe the three principles of justice the commentary identifies:

6. Verses 19-20 articulate what has come to be known as the principle of *lex talionis*, a Roman legal term referring to equal justice being done; it essentially means the punishment must fit the crime. Describe in your own words the "limiting" effect of the "eye for an eye" principle:

7. How was the "eye for an eye" principle of justice applied differently in Israel than in other ancient Near Eastern cultures, due to Israel's understanding (from Moses' teaching in Genesis) that all people are created in God's image?

8. In his Sermon on the Mount, Jesus corrected a first-century misapplication of the "eye for eye" principle. He taught that in personal relationships, it is not equal justice that applies, but rather the law of love and forgiveness, which prompts us to be generous with others even when we have been wronged or when there is no chance of being repaid (295). How do some commentators believe the first-century Jews were misapplying the "eye for eye" principle?

APPLY

A. Acknowledging the Lord's Continual Presence—By keeping the lamps burning continually each night and placing fresh cakes of the bread of the Presence before the Lord each Sabbath, the priests acknowledged his continual presence with them in his holy dwelling (288-89). In the new covenant ushered in by Jesus Christ, the very bodies of his followers are the Lord's holy dwelling place (1 Cor 6:19-20). **Given that reality, write down two or three practical ways you can acknowledge and revere the Lord's continual presence with you if you are a follower of Jesus:**

B. Affirming Our Willingness to Serve the Lord Always—The other thing the priests did by continually keeping the lamps burning and the bread of the Presence on the table was to affirm their willingness to serve the Lord always (288, 290). Today we are called to continually serve King Jesus, surrendering our very lives to the one who is worthy of all we have (Mt 16:24-26). Serving the Lord can be done only with a whole heart, or it can't be done at all (Mt 6:24; 10:37-39). **Take a few moments to reflect on the things that may be preventing you from serving the Lord with a whole heart. Write down two or three that you want to commit to the Lord in prayer and actively work to change:**

RESPOND

Meditate—One of the lessons we can draw from Leviticus 24 is that the Lord is pleased by even the most mundane activities if they are done out of reverence for his holiness. Keeping lamps burning and a table set with fresh bread were, in some ways, quite ordinary tasks for the Israelite priests. Yet the Lord established these ordinary tasks as continual rites for his most holy dwelling. As you go about the ordinary tasks of your life this week, mediate on Col 3:23-24: "Whatever you do, work at it with all your heart, as working for the Lord and not for others, knowing that you will receive an inheritance from the Lord as your reward. It is the Lord Christ you are serving."

Take Action—As you meditate on Col 3:23-24 this week, be mindful of your heart attitude as you work on the ordinary tasks before you. Pick one or two, and pray before you begin them that the Lord would help you see their holiness as you work at them with all your heart for him. Take a few notes on how those experiences felt, especially the extent to which they helped you be more aware of and reverent toward the Lord's presence.

Continual Rites in the Holy Place, and Revering the Lord's Holy Name

---

ANALYZE

Opening Prayer

Heavenly Father, as we study your word in Leviticus, help us to become more continually aware of your presence with us at all times, and your indwelling presence in our hearts through your Holy Spirit. Strengthen our wills to continually serve you by surrendering our lives to your Son, our Lord Jesus, in whose name we pray. Amen.

Share Reflections | 5 min.

Have each person share one reflection from the Reflect exercise on the first page of the Individual Study. You can do this in pairs, or in the larger group if you have time. This is not a time to critique or ask lots of questions of each other, but simply to share something God has put on your heart.

Clarify Issues from the Lesson | 10 min.

Back in the larger group, prepare for your discussion by clarifying any uncertainties about the Scripture or commentary, but be careful with your time. The purpose here is to focus on a few issues that may be particularly difficult, not to open a broad discussion about the lesson.

Meaning of Leviticus for Today | 20 min.

Take turns reading aloud each point below, and discuss the questions as a group:

A. Continually Reaffirming Our Covenant Commitments—By placing the bread of the Presence before the Lord every Sabbath as a covenant sign (Lev 24:8), the priests continually reaffirmed the people's covenant commitment to the Lord and continually requested his covenant favor (290). Although we no longer perform these Levitical rites, the New Testament ordinance of the Lord's Supper accomplishes these same purposes (see Mt 26:26-29; Lk 22:17-20; 1 Cor 11:23-26). **What are some additional ways a church, small group, family, or other forms of Christian community might regularly reaffirm their covenant commitment to the Lord and request his covenant favor?**

B. Blaspheming the Name of the Lord—Leviticus 24 narrates an episode in which a man cursed the Lord's name—an act of blasphemy. Capital punishment is no longer applicable for this offense among God's people (see Introduction, 57-62), but blasphemy is and will always be a serious offense against the Lord (see Ex 20:7; 1 Cor 15:15; 1 Tim 1:13, 20; Jas 2:7; 2 Pet 2:12). While the guilt of the man who cursed the Lord's name in Leviticus 24 is obvious to us, we can be oblivious to the many subtle ways in which we take the Lord's name in vain or otherwise treat his sacred things with contempt. **Discuss some of the ways this may happen in contemporary Christian communities, and with individual Christians:**

EVALUATE

Christian Advocacy for Justice | 20 min.

The principles of justice set forth in Lev 24:17-22 underscore the high value of human life (vv. 17-18, 21), the importance of penalties fitting the crime (vv. 19-20), and the equality of all people under the law (v. 22). Followers of Jesus should be at the forefront of advocating for justice in our communities, country, and around the world (cf. Isa 1:17; 16:3; 42:1; Jer 22:3; Amos 5:24; Mic 6:8; Mt 12:20; 23:23; Lk 11:42; Jas 2:1-4). **Evaluate how well you think the Church is doing in advocating for justice around the world. Consider both its excellent efforts in many places and on many issues, as well as those places or issues where Christians seem to turn a blind eye to justice. Discuss steps your own church or small group might take to make even a small advance in Christian advocacy for justice:**

Laws for the Sabbath and Jubilee Years and for Redeeming People and Property

ENGAGE

Reflect

Reflect on the busyness of your life and how you feel about taking a weekly Sabbath break from your work. Does the idea of keeping a regular Sabbath make you anxious? If so, why? Are you so burned out from work that you should probably take a full sabbatical for several weeks or even months? What would keep you from doing that? If you do take a weekly Sabbath, is it actually restful? How might you change your Sabbath practices so you are resting as the Lord intends?

Pray

Heavenly Father, as I study your word in Leviticus, help me to trust in your care for me and my family and in your promise to provide for our basic life needs. Help me to trust you to the point that I can engage all the more in keeping a regular Sabbath to refresh my body and soul and enjoy your presence with me. I pray these things in Jesus' name. Amen.

Read

- Read Leviticus 25, which concerns laws for the Israelites to keep a Sabbath year to let the people and land rest and a Jubilee year every fiftieth year to forgive debts and give families a fresh start.
- In the commentary, read the preface (296-97) and "Context" (297-99).
- Read Leviticus 25 again.

UNDERSTAND

A. Laws for Sabbath and Jubilee Years—Read "Comments" on Lev 25:1-22 and "Meaning" (299-303). The laws in verses 1-7 concern the Sabbath year (every seventh year); the laws in vv. 8-17 concern the Jubilee year (every fiftieth year); vv. 18-22 conclude this section.

1. When the Israelites took possession of the Promised Land, every seven years they were to observe a Sabbath year of not working the land so it could rest. What were they permitted to do with the land during this seventh year, and what were they forbidden from doing?

2. In what two significant ways did the Sabbath year parallel the Sabbath day?

3. Because the Israelites' harvests in the year after the Sabbath year were not guaranteed by nature to be good ones, letting the land rest for an entire year was a bold proclamation. What were they proclaiming?

4. One practical result of the Jubilee year was to liberate, or free, the people by releasing them from debts that had forced them to sell their land or themselves. What did this mean for the Israelites?

5. Other ancient Near Eastern sources mention similar proclamations of "release," but they were very different than Israel's Jubilee. Describe the differences between other ancient Near Eastern practices and the Lord's proclamation of release in the Jubilee:

6. Israelites who had "sold" their land to pay for debts were allowed to return and take full possession in the Year of Jubilee. Why then is "leasing" rather than "selling" the land a better description of the Israelites' practice?

7. Verses 18-19 refer to the people living safely in the land and eating their fill, a promise from the Lord to provide for the needs of his people basic to abundant human life. What picture emerges from this promise?

B. Redemption and Jubilee for the Poor—Read "Comments" on Lev 25:23-55 and "Meaning" (303-12). This section explains how redemption and Jubilee worked for those forced by poverty to sell their property (via leases) or themselves.

1. The Lord prohibited the permanent sale of land among the Israelites and gave them the right to redeem any land they had sold at any time. What danger did these laws address?

2. When poverty forced Israelites to sell (that is, lease) some of their property to pay debts, they had three options for redeeming the land from the buyer. Briefly describe those three options:

3. If Israelites became so indebted they had to sell all their land to pay creditors, the community was to "support" them (v. 35). Creditors were not to oppress their fellow Israelites. Briefly describe how the Lord expected creditors to support their poor fellow Israelites and what they were prohibited from doing:

4. When Israelites became so poor that they had sold all their property but were still in debt, their last resort was to sell themselves, either to a fellow Israelite or a resident alien. But the Lord prohibited permanent servitude (unless voluntary; see Dt 15:12-17). If, by the Year of Jubilee, impoverished Israelites had not earned enough money to fully pay their debts or had not been redeemed by a relative, they were released from their servitude. What is the theological reason an Israelite could not be sold as a permanent slave?

5. Our English term "slave" is potentially misleading in the context of Leviticus. We tend to think of slaves in terms of the brutal slavery of the Greco-Roman world or modern slavery in Europe and the United States, in which a slave is considered a piece of legal property, bound to absolute obedience, to be treated any way the owner desires. But this type of slavery was forbidden to the Israelites. Briefly describe in your own words why this was the case:

6. The commentary points out that a relationship of power is not necessarily dehumanizing, depending on how that relationship is exercised (309). Briefly describe the two points the commentary makes concerning indentured and permanent servitude:

7. The Year of Jubilee emphasizes the Lord's priorities for humanity. The first priority concerns *economics* and the importance of *equity* and *opportunity*. Briefly describe in your own words these two facets of the Lord's priority of economics:

A. Protecting the Family Unit—For his people to live in close relationships with their families is important to the Lord; he has appointed the family as the foundation of society (298). One of the purposes of Leviticus 25 is to ensure the Israelites maintained close family relationships by reducing the threat indebtedness posed to the health and stability of families (298). To this day, debt is a significant cause of family disruption, crime, poverty, violence, and other social ills (311). By cancelling all debts, the Year of Jubilee aimed to avert these social ills, reunite families, and provide them with a fresh start for prospering together on their own land (312). **Take some time to reflect on your own financial situation (or your family's, if you're currently part of a family economic unit). How is debt affecting your personal or family health and well-being? Have you looked into any resources for helping you manage your finances, especially reducing your debt? What are some concrete steps you can take to start reducing your financial debt?**

B. Sabbath Rest for the Lord's People—The Sabbath law of Leviticus 25 benefited the Israelites by providing rest from back-breaking agricultural work. They were also to keep the command as a way of honoring their covenant relationship with the Lord (299) (see Ex 31:13, 16; Lev 16:31). While it is debated whether the Sabbath command still applies to Christians today, the fact remains that, as with all of the Ten Commandments, Sabbath-keeping (Ex 20:8-11) reflects the values of the Lord, who himself rested from his work in creation and declared that resting holy (Gen 2:1-3). He models and values regular rest. **If you don't keep a weekly Sabbath now, what are some concrete ways you might benefit from starting this practice? Whether or not you keep a weekly Sabbath now, what are some concrete steps you might take to help keep it more regularly and honor it as holy to the Lord?**

RESPOND

Meditate—When the Israelites allowed the land to rest in the Sabbath and Jubilee years, they were proclaiming their faith in the Lord's care and provision for their needs (300, 303). Jesus echoes this same call to faith in the New Testament when he commands us to not be anxious about our lives, but to seek first God's kingdom and his righteousness (Mt 6:25-33). Meditate this week on Mt 6:25-33 and the Lord's promise to take care of our earthly needs as we seek first his kingdom and righteousness in how we live.

Take Action—As you meditate on Mt 6:25-33 this week, be mindful of your anxieties about life and the degree to which you are trusting the Lord to care for your basic needs. Journal in the space below how you are feeling about these things, and perhaps write a prayer asking the Lord to encourage and strengthen your faith in his promise to care for you.

LAWS FOR THE SABBATH AND JUBILEE YEARS AND FOR REDEEMING PEOPLE AND PROPERTY

ENGAGE

Reflect

Heavenly Father, as we study your word in Leviticus, help us to trust in your care for us and our families and in your promise to provide for our basic life needs. Help us to trust you to the point that we can engage all the more in keeping a regular Sabbath rest to refresh our bodies and souls and enjoy your presence with us. We pray these things in Jesus' name. Amen.

Share Reflections | 5 min.

Have each person share one reflection from the Reflect exercise on the first page of the Individual Study. You can do this in pairs, or in the larger group if you have time. This is not a time to critique or ask lots of questions of each other, but simply to share something God has put on your heart.

Clarify Issues from the Lesson | 10 min.

Back in the larger group, prepare for your discussion by clarifying any uncertainties about the Scripture or commentary, but be careful with your time. The purpose here is to focus on a few issues that may be particularly difficult, not to open a broad discussion about the lesson.

Meaning of Leviticus for Today | 20 min.

Take turns reading aloud each point below, and discuss the questions as a group:

A. The Lord's Priorities for Economic Equity and Opportunity—The law of the Year of Jubilee stresses the importance to the Lord of both economic equity and opportunity. The *equity* envisioned by the Lord's values reflected in this law is neither socialism (the Israelites owned their land) nor unchecked *capitalism* (the Jubilee prevented a wealthy few from accumulating most of the land). Instead, the Jubilee reflects the creation principle that God has given the earth to all humanity, and we are all called to act responsibly and ethically as co-stewards of its resources (311). Likewise, the Jubilee provided both *opportunity* and supporting resources for families to have a fresh start on their own land by cancelling indebtedness (311). **What are some policies in our society and other societies that operate against these priorities of the Lord? What are some concrete, practical ways Christians can promote the kind of societies here and in other countries that reflect his priorities?**

B. Devastation of Debt—Leviticus 25 aims to avert some of the devastating social consequences of indebtedness, which is a significant cause of family disruption, crime, poverty, and violence in our culture. **Discuss some practical steps your church or small group might take to identify and help those struggling with debt in your community to begin to free themselves from its devastating effects. What principles in Leviticus 25 might be helpful in this regard?**

EVALUATE

Freedom from Modern Slavery

The servitude envisioned in Leviticus 25 is nothing like our notions of modern slavery, with its treatment of human beings as legal property, bound to absolute obedience, and subject to any kind of treatment the slave owner desires. Indeed, the Israelites were forbidden from such practice (308). In the last few years, we in the West have been gaining more insight and awareness about modern slavery as it continues around the world and in our own country to this day. **Spend some time in your large or small groups evaluating what you know about modern human trafficking and the resources and organizations working against this evil in your own community and around the world. Take some steps to share relevant information and local contacts with one another. Consider participating personally in an anti-trafficking organization or activity.**

COVENANT BLESSINGS AND CURSES

ENGAGE

Reflect

Reflect on whether and to what extent you consider your life to be blessed. Why do you feel that way? Do you feel as though the Lord himself has blessed you? In what ways? Are you able to give him thanks for those blessings? On the other hand, do you feel as though the Lord has withheld blessings from your life in certain ways? What are those ways? How do you feel about that?

Pray

Heavenly Father, as I study your word in Leviticus, help me to see the many blessings you have bestowed on me and my loved ones. Help me to know that your blessings are not because I have earned your favor, but because you have graciously shown me your love through my faith in your Son Jesus, in whose name I give you thanks and pray. Amen.

Read

- Read Leviticus 26, which highlights the blessings that would come to Israel for embracing their covenant with the Lord from the heart and the curses that would come from rejecting the covenant.
- In the commentary, read "Context" (313-14).
- Read Leviticus 26 again.

UNDERSTAND

A. Blessings for Obedience to the Covenant—Read "Comments" on Lev 26:1-13 (314-17).

1. The introduction (vv. 1-2) is a general call to Israel to covenant faithfulness. It includes one prohibition and two positive commands. Briefly describe them in your own words:

2. Following the general call to faithfulness in vv. 1-2, the next section (vv. 3-13) is clear that such faithfulness is a necessary condition for Israel to experience covenant blessings. Explain why it would be a misunderstanding to read this text as describing a relationship with the Lord earned through obedience:

3. The blessings of vv. 4-12 fall under two categories. Briefly describe these two categories:

4. The second category addresses the very thing the human soul needs most: relationship with the Lord himself. Why does the commentary suggest this blessing is listed last?

5. The language of verse 9 echoes the covenant promises the Lord made to Abraham and his descendants, the Israelites. What is the Lord indicating by fulfilling these promises?

6. The blessings described in vv. 3-10 would essentially make the land like the garden of Eden. Verses 11-12 then return to the Lord's goal in Eden: walking among his people as their God. Briefly describe the five examples of this goal depicted in the Bible after the first glimpse in Gen 3:8:

B. Curses for Rejecting the Covenant—Read "Comments" on Lev 26:14-39 (317-22).

1. The curses described here are not petty acts of anger by the Lord. How does the commentary describe the curses?

2. The commentary notes that many of the curses in Leviticus 26 are exact opposites of its blessings. Review the chart on p. 317 and briefly describe in your own words the four categories of contrasting blessings and curses:

3. The curses of Leviticus 26 were not intended to punish the Israelites for failing to perfectly keep the law; when they did sin, the Lord had mercifully provided atoning sacrifices (Lev 4-5) and the Day of Atonement (Lev 16). Instead, the curses were intended to discipline the Israelites for completely rejecting their covenant relationship with the Lord through gross disobedience. What analogy does the commentary give for the mistake some people today make in taking a negative view of the Lord bringing these curses to bear?

4. The commentary points out (319) that the Lord's discipline often begins by breaking us of our stubborn pride. How might his covenant blessings have led the Israelites to such pride?

5. In verse 2, the Lord commanded Israel to revere his sanctuary, yet in v. 31a, he promises as a curse to "lay waste" (NIV) or "make desolate" (ESV) their sanctuaries. Whether this refers to idolatrous places of worship or to authorized sanctuaries of the Lord is debated. Either way, it emphasizes he would "take no delight" in their offerings. Why would he reject the Israelites' offerings in this case?

6. Exile to another land was a horrible curse for Israel because possession of the land was central to the covenant promises (Gen 112:1, 7; 15:18). What was signified by the Israelites remaining in the land and, alternately, being exiled from the land?

C. Mercy to a Repentant People—Read "Comments" on Lev 26:40-46 and "Meaning" (322-25).

1. Circumcision was the sign of the covenant in the Old Testament. To have an "uncircumcised heart" (v. 41) was therefore to have a heart that rejected the covenant. How does the commentary explain the significance of an uncircumcised heart?

2. In v. 42, the Lord promises to "remember" his covenant with Jacob, Isaac, and Abraham in response to the Israelites humbling their hearts and undergoing his discipline. This does not imply the Lord would ever forget his covenant, but that he would fulfill its promises. What is the clear implication of v. 42?

3. As we've seen, the blessings of Leviticus 26 would ensure the Israelites would walk in rich fellowship with their divine King, like a return to the garden of Eden. How was Israel privileged in connection with this promise of blessing?

4. The lists of blessings of Leviticus 26 begin with material things and culminate with the greatest blessing of all: relationship with God himself. How did Jesus emphasize this same priority?

APPLY

A. The Lord's Discipline Against Our Pride—The Lord promises to discipline us in increasing ways when he sees we are bound by our stubborn pride and think we have no need of him or his ways. Sometimes, even the blessings the Lord bestows on us can lead to pride when we forget they come from his hand and not from our own competence and accomplishments. (319). **Take time to reflect on your relationship with God in terms of what might be his discipline in your life. Are there aspects of your life in which you feel he's "let you down" or, even worse, "cursed" you? Is it possible that any of these involve your pride in ways that may have caused you to turn away from relying on him? Can you see any ways in which he might actually be calling you to a deeper relationship of trust and dependence by frustrating your efforts to "go it alone"?**

B. Humbling Our "Uncircumcised" Hearts—The Lord promised Israel he would remember his covenant if they would humble their uncircumcised hearts, which refers to hearts not wholly committed to their covenant with him. **Are there any areas in your life where your heart is not wholly committed to your relationship with the Lord? If so, why isn't it? How do you feel about "turning" toward the Lord and "walking" with him more closely in these areas (Lev 26:23)? To the extent you desire to do that, what are some practical steps you might take?**

RESPOND

Meditate—Leviticus 26 depicts God's promise that we will be blessed by obeying his word. But we should not confuse this with the false idea that our obedience somehow earns a right standing with the Lord. Only our union with Christ and reliance upon his atoning sacrifice brings us into right standing with God because Jesus' right standing is given to us by God's grace through faith (Eph 2:8). Our obedience is an act of grateful worship in response to that grace and an acknowledgement that we want to honor our redeeming King and continue in fellowship with him (315). In that light, meditate this week on the Lord's words to us in Jn 14:15: "If you love me, you will keep my commands."

Take Action—As you meditate on Jn 14:15 this week, be mindful of those areas in your life where there may be opportunity to excel all the more in loving the Lord Jesus by following harder after his ways. Take time during the week to note any of those areas, and take a few practical steps toward loving him more deeply through obedience, paying attention to any blessings you may experience as a result.

COVENANT BLESSINGS AND CURSES

ENGAGE

Opening Prayer

Heavenly Father, as we study your word in Leviticus, help us to see the many blessings you have bestowed on us and our loved ones. Help us to know that your blessings are not because we have earned your favor, but because you have graciously shown us your love through our faith in your Son Jesus, in whose name we give you thanks and pray. Amen.

Share Reflections | 5 min.

Have each person share one reflection from the Reflect exercise on the first page of the Individual Study. You can do this in pairs, or in the larger group if you have time. This is not a time to critique or ask lots of questions of each other, but simply to share something God has put on your heart.

Clarify Issues from the Lesson | 10 min.

Back in the larger group, prepare for your discussion by clarifying any uncertainties about the Scripture or commentary, but be careful with your time. The purpose here is to focus on a few issues that may be particularly difficult, not to open a broad discussion about the lesson.

Meaning of Leviticus for Today | 20 min.

Take turns reading aloud each point below, and discuss the questions as a group:

A. Responding to the Prosperity Gospel—The "prosperity gospel" is a false teaching that has gained popularity in the West and other parts of the world, including Africa. In essence, it teaches that the Lord will bring financial security or even wealth to those who show sufficient faith. Often the first evidence of "faith" the false teachers suggest is to make a financial offering to their ministry: the larger the offering, the greater the demonstration of faith. Most of all, this teaching emphasizes material blessings as the supreme goal and greatest good in life. **How does this compare to Leviticus 26 (see p. 315)? Discuss any "ministries," churches, or other organizations that may be promoting the prosperity gospel. Analyze why you think this may be the case. Be sure to keep your discussion gracious and open-minded, especially if anyone in your group disagrees or has been giving financial support to such a ministry. To the extent you agree that any given "ministry" is teaching falsely about the Lord's material blessings, how might you explain this to others by what you have learned in Leviticus 26?**

B. Tangible Signs of the Covenant—Among the curses for breaking the covenant was the threat Israel would be exiled from the land, which was central to the covenant promises God had made to Abraham, Isaac, and Jacob. But as long as Israel remained in the land, they had at least one tangible sign that their covenant relationship with the Lord was on good terms (321). **Read Lk 22:14-20 and Rom 6:3-5. God has given us the ordinances of the Lord's Supper and baptism as tangible signs or symbols of his new covenant with us in the death and resurrection of his Son Jesus. How have you seen some churches practice these ordinances in ways that especially remind the community of our covenant relationship with the Lord? What are some other ways a church might practice the Lord's Supper and baptism to emphasize even further these tangible signs of the Lord's covenant with us?**

EVALUATE

Remembering the Land | 20 min.

The Lord created and commissioned us to rule over the earth justly (Gen 1:26-28), since it is the object of his special care (cf. Lev 25:1-7). For the Israelites, this meant letting it "rest" every seven years. If they failed to do so (vv. 2, 34-35, 43), the Lord would "remember the land" (v. 42), which in this case means caring for it by sending his people into exile so that it could have a proper rest (323). **Evaluate the ways the peoples of the world, especially the Western world, have "violated the land's Sabbaths," so to speak. How have we failed to respect the earth and its natural resources (including plant and animal life) in ways that violate our commission as God's representatives to care for them? How has this violation of our commission harmed our fellow man? What** are some current and past practices of carefully managing natural resources that demonstrate the Sabbath principle that "resting the land"—trusting God with the results of creation care—actually yields greater production of higher-quality resources? How might we as Christians change our own behaviors and attempt to influence others toward this kind of creation care?

LAWS CONCERNING DEDICATION AND REDEMPTION OF PERSONS OR PROPERTY VOWED TO THE LORD

ENGAGE

Reflect

If you are a follower of Jesus, what is your discipleship costing you, not just financially, but in other ways as well? Likewise, if you worship God corporately in a local church and bring financial offerings to him, how much are those costing you? What about the offerings of your time and talents to the church? How much are they costing you? Do your financial offerings come from your excess discretionary earnings or do they cause you to trust in the Lord for his future provision because they are such costly gifts? How do you feel about the assessment you have just made? Does it prompt you to make any changes? Why or why not?

Pray

Heavenly Father, as I study your word in Leviticus, empower me by your Holy Spirit to have the will and strength to fulfill your calling on my life to serve and worship you wholeheartedly, no matter the cost to me. I thank you for your grace and provision in my life. I give this thanks and pray in Jesus' name. Amen.

Read

- Read Leviticus 27. This final chapter focuses on redemption, as did Chapter 25. The primary context here concerns the redemption of persons or property the Israelites had vowed to dedicate to the Lord. Making vows helped the Israelites express the seriousness of their prayers, and fulfilling those vows helped ensure they would give him thanks for answering them. But sometimes they made vows rashly—such as vowing to dedicate a child to the Lord's service in the sanctuary—and later sought to be released from it. So the Lord provided a gracious means in Leviticus 27 to redeem persons or property vowed to him by paying an amount equal to their value into the sanctuary. For example, vv. 2-8 concern the redemption values for persons dedicated to the Lord by vows. Note this situation was not one in which an Israelite had vowed the *value* of a person (so some versions, v. 2), but had vowed to dedicate the *person* (see NKJV, v. 2).

- In the commentary, read "Context" (326).
- Read Leviticus 27 again.

UNDERSTAND

A. Laws Concerning Voluntary Vow Offerings—Read "Comments" on Lev 27:1-24 (326-330), and "Comment" on vow offerings at Lev 7:16-18 (135).

1. The assumption throughout Leviticus 27 is that vows made to the Lord must be honored. What is the rationale for this assumption?

2. The provisions of vv. 1-8 allowed an Israelite to redeem from a "special vow" a person they had dedicated to the Lord's service. In what way was this law particularly compassionate?

3. This first section of vv. 1-8 provides "valuations" (or perhaps better, "assessments") of certain persons by age and sex. In our modern way of thinking, we may be tempted to conclude these valuations reflected the intrinsic worth of the persons (for example, males were considered more valuable than females). But this makes no sense of the text. What example and argument does the commentary give to explain why these assessments do <u>not</u> concern intrinsic worth?

4. If the valuations or assessments of Lev 27:1-8 do not concern intrinsic worth of persons, what is the better explanation, and why is it better?

5. Verse 8 provides that if an Israelite was too poor to afford the standard assessment for redeeming a person they had vowed, the priests would give an assessment according to what the vower could afford. What, in his grace, was the Lord making way for here?

6. Verses 9-13 turn to the subject of redeeming animals vowed to the Lord. Only those animals considered ceremonially *unclean* could be redeemed (vv. 11-13). If an Israelite vowed a ceremonially clean animal, it could not be redeemed but had to be sacrificed as a vow offering (see Lev. 7:16-18). Furthermore, the Israelite was prohibited from exchanging it with an unclean animal or substituting a clean animal of lesser value. What human tendency did this law therefore deter? How?

7. Verses 14-24 turn to the subject of redeeming non-living property, specifically houses and land. In vv. 16-19, when an Israelite vowed to dedicate his land, he did not immediately give it to the priests because they did not have time to care for it and because the land was still redeemable. How could an Israelite redeem land he had vowed to the Lord?

8. What happened to land vowed to the Lord if the owner failed to redeem it?

9. What happened to land vowed to the Lord if the owner then leased ("sold") it to someone else, and why was that the result?

B. Laws Concerning Non-Voluntary Offerings and Non-Redeemable Persons and Property— Read "Comments" on Lev 27:26-33 (330-33). Leviticus 27:2-24 concerns voluntary vow offerings that could be dedicated to the Lord but that were normally redeemable. This section, vv. 26-33, concerns *involuntary* offerings—things that *could not be dedicated* to fulfill a vow because they were already the Lord's (firstborn, tithes)—and people and property that could be dedicated to him but *could not be redeemed* (called "devoted" things).

1. Leviticus reflects the theological reality that all firstborn Israelite males, human or animal, belonged to the Lord as holy. What was the historical background to this reality?

2. An Israelite could not vow to dedicate an animal he owned and then attempt to pay that vow with a firstborn animal (since the firstborn of all ceremonially clean animals already belonged to the Lord). What analogy does the commentary give for such an attempt?

3. Verses 28-29 concern persons or property that could not be redeemed because they had been irrevocably "devoted" to the Lord, either by vow (v. 28) or because of the Lord's command (v. 29). In the first case, the person making the vow intended to underscore the extreme seriousness of their prayers and their degree of thankfulness by promising to give the person or property to the Lord permanently – not by merely dedicating their service or value to the Lord for a time. In the case of devoted persons, what did this likely entail?

4. Verse 29 deals with very limited and precise contexts in which the Lord had commanded or agreed certain people or their property be destroyed because of his judgment against them for their wickedness. This was

restricted to certain specific acts of war against evil nations (see Num 21:2; Josh 6:17; 1 Sam 15:3; Deut 20:10-18) or to judgment against Israelites themselves who practiced idolatry (see Exod 22:20; Deut 13:13-16). The Bible clearly teaches the Lord will bring his justice to bear against human evil at the end of time; the above cases were instances of this end-time judgment breaking into human history, with Israel as his instrument delivering his justice (331, esp. n. 6). How do we know this verse does <u>not</u> permit an individual Israelite to irrevocably devote his children or servants to the Lord and then kill them in payment of the vow?

5. Verses 30-33 concern laws of the tithe, the provision of 10 percent of the Israelites' agricultural production to the Lord for the service of his tabernacle. As with the ceremonial clean firstborn animals, the tithes of produce could not be dedicated to the Lord in fulfillment of a vow because they already belonged to him (they were "holy to the Lord"–vv. 30, 32). One gracious exception existed: An Israelite was permitted to redeem a portion of his tithe of plant crops (not animals, see vv. 32-33) if his harvest was so small he needed to keep back some for food and seed (v. 31). How did the tithe meet the needs of those who served at the tabernacle and the needy in Israel?

APPLY

Read "Meaning" (334-35).

A. Promising God Much, Thanking Him Little—Lev 27:9-10 prohibited an Israelite from vowing to give a ceremonially clean animal to the Lord and then trying to fulfill that vow with either an unclean animal or a clean animal of lesser value. The law forbade this kind of ingratitude by deeming *both animals* holy, thus preventing the vower from keeping either. Our human tendency is to promise God much when we need him but thank him little once he's met our needs. **What are some typical situations in contemporary American life in which we may be tempted to treat the Lord this way? Have you ever done this or heard of someone who has? What did the situation involve?**

B. Giving to the Lord in Ways that Cost Us Little—In a similar way, Lev 27:20-21 prevented Israelites from vowing their land, leasing it to someone else, and then redeeming it with money. If they attempted this, the land became the permanent possession of the priests for the benefit of the sanctuary. This was most likely intended to prevent people from redeeming land with money they had done virtually nothing to earn (since the lessee had done all the hard work producing crops from the land). **How might Christians today fall into this same temptation to worship the Lord with our material gifts in ways that cost us little? What might be some safeguards against this temptation?**

RESPOND

Meditate—Although making vows to the Lord is not a common New Testament practice—and Scripture actually warns against its risks (Eccl 5:5)—Christians are nevertheless under obligation to the Lord to fulfill the calling he has made on our lives (Gal 5:14; 6:2; Eph 4:1-3; 1 Thess 4:7-8; 2 Thess 1:11-12; 1 Pet 1:14-16; 2:20-21; 3:9). Meditate this week on 2 Thess 1:11-12: "With this in mind, we constantly pray for you, that our God may make you worthy of his calling, and that by his power he may bring to fruition your every desire for goodness and your every deed prompted by faith. We pray this so that the name of our Lord Jesus may be glorified in you, and you in him, according to the grace of our God and the Lord Jesus Christ."

Take Action—A consistent theme in Leviticus 27 is that our worship should be costly to reflect our thanks for the great debt the Lord has removed from us through the atoning sacrifice of Jesus for our sins. Jesus applies this same theme to discipleship and warns that we who would commit our lives to him should not do so lightly, but only if we follow him wholeheartedly: There is no turning back (Lk 9:61-62; 14:25-33). Reflect on your commitment to following Jesus and the areas in your life where you are not pursuing that commitment with your whole heart. What changes will you need to make to follow Jesus wholeheartedly? In what ways and to what extent will those changes be costly to you? How do you feel about giving Jesus such costly commitment and worship?

LEVITICUS 27

LAWS CONCERNING DEDICATION AND REDEMPTION OF PERSONS OR PROPERTY VOWED TO THE LORD

ANALYZE

Opening Prayer

Heavenly Father, as we study your word in Leviticus, empower us by your Holy Spirit to have the will and strength to fulfill your calling on our lives to serve and worship you wholeheartedly, no matter the cost to us. We thank you for your grace and provision in our lives. We give this thanks and pray in Jesus' name. Amen.

Share Reflections | 5 min.

Have each person share one reflection from the Reflect exercise on the first page of the Individual Study. You can do this in pairs, or in the larger group if you have time. This is not a time to critique or ask lots of questions of each other, but simply to share something God has put on your heart.

Clarify Issues from the Lesson | 10 min.

Back in the larger group, prepare for your discussion by clarifying any uncertainties about the Scripture or commentary, but be careful with your time. The purpose here is to focus on a few issues that may be particularly difficult, not to open a broad discussion about the lesson.

Meaning of Leviticus for Today | 20 min.

Take turns reading aloud each point below, and discuss the questions as a group:

A. Accommodating Our Worship for Everyone's Participation—Levitcus 27:8 provided that Israelites too poor to pay the full redemption value for a person they had vowed to dedicate would be assessed a redemption value in keeping with their ability to pay. This was the Lord's way of ensuring that all people, whether rich or poor, could participate fully in worshipping him—in this case, by enabling them to fulfill their vow. **What are some ways you have seen churches or other Christian communities fail to accommodate their worship practices or other gatherings so that all might participate fully? Consider the many ways beyond economic barriers in which**

people might be hindered from fully participating in worship. What are some safeguards a Church or other Christian community might take to accommodate their practices so that everyone can participate fully?

B. Tithing to Support the Poor—The tithe of Leviticus 27 was extended in Deut 14:28-29 beyond providing for the priests to caring for the financially needy. The New Testament continues this same principle, applying it fundamentally to caring for the needy within the church itself (Rom 15:25-27; 1 Cor 16:1-3; 2 Cor 8:1-15). **What are some ways your own church or community is already providing for the needy through the financial gifts of its members? What more do you see that could be done, and how? How might your church provide for the needy in the larger community and also follow the biblical priority of giving to the poor who are followers of Jesus?**

EVALUATE

Setting Apart Our Children to the Lord | 20 min.

In some churches, parents baptize their infants, understanding baptism to be the sign of the new covenant and thus following the biblical model of applying the covenant sign to their children (see Gen 17:10-12). In doing so, they mark the child as set apart to the Lord. In other churches, parents publicly dedicate infants and young children to the Lord, modeling their practice after the story of Hannah dedicating her son, Samuel, to the Lord (see 1 Sam 1:21-28). There Hannah proclaimed, "I have lent him to the Lord. As long as he lives, he is lent to the Lord" (1 Sam 21:28). **Whether parents in your church set infants apart to the Lord through baptism or a dedication service, what are some practical ways parents and their church communities can fulfill the commitment they have made to set these children apart to the Lord? In other words, if you were to make a vow to the Lord to set apart your children to him (either your own children or spiritual children in the larger community), what would you do specifically to fulfill that vow?**

Printed in Great Britain
by Amazon

46995764R00132